Certified Tester Advanced Level

Test Analyst

Daniel Hângan

Copyright © 2024 Daniel Hângan

All rights reserved

- Do you love to have paper books at home?
- Do you have two dollars to pay for the printing of this book?
- Do you have two dollars to pay for my work?
- Do you have two more dollars for other costs?

- You are the winner! This book is yours!

- This book was made by combining the Syllabus v3.1.2 2022 pdf file, the Sample Exam Questions v2.6 pdf file and the Sample Exam Answers v2.6 pdf file.

- This book was made for people that love to have paper books.

- There is no extra information added by the author. Only some changes to some pages to fit in the book.

Certified Tester Advanced Level Test Analyst (CTAL-TA) Syllabus

v3.1.2

International Software Testing Qualifications Board

ISTQB®
Certified Tester
Advanced Level
Test Analyst

Certified Tester Advanced Level
Test Analyst (CTAL-TA)

Copyright Notice © International Software Testing Qualifications Board (hereinafter called ISTQB®) ISTQB® is a registered trademark of the International Software Testing Qualifications Board.

Copyright © 2021-2022 the authors of the update v3.1.0, errata 3.1.1 and errata 3.1.2: Wim Decoutere, István Forgács, Matthias Hamburg, Adam Roman, Jan Sabak, Marc-Florian Wendland.

Copyright © 2019 the authors of the update 2019: Graham Bath, Judy McKay, Jan Sabak, Erik van Veenendaal

Copyright © 2012 the authors: Judy McKay, Mike Smith, Erik van Veenendaal

All rights reserved.The authors hereby transfer the copyright to the ISTQB®. The authors (as current copyright holders) and ISTQB® (as the future copyright holder) have agreed to the following conditions of use:

Extracts, for non-commercial use, from this document may be copied if the source is acknowledged.Any Accredited Training Provider may use this syllabus as the basis for a training course if the authors and the ISTQB® are acknowledged as the source and copyright owners of the syllabus and provided that any advertisement of such a training course may mention the syllabus only after official Accreditation of the training materials has been received from an ISTQB®-recognized Member Board.

Any individual or group of individuals may use this syllabus as the basis for articles and books, if the authors and the ISTQB® are acknowledged as the source and copyright owners of the syllabus.

Any other use of this syllabus is prohibited without first obtaining the approval in writing of the ISTQB®.

Any ISTQB®-recognized Member Board may translate this syllabus provided they reproduce the abovementioned Copyright Notice in the translated version of the syllabus.

Certified Tester Advanced Level
Test Analyst (CTAL-TA)

Revision History

Version	Date	Remarks
2012 v2.0	2012/10/19	First version as a separate AL-TA Syllabus
2019 v3.0	2019/10/19	Major update with overall revision and scope reduction
v3.1.0	2021/03/03	Minor update with section 3.2.3 rewritten and various wording improvements
v3.1.1	2021/05/15	Errata: The copyright notice has been adapted to the current ISTQB® standards.
v3.1.2	2022/01/31	Errata: Minor formatting, grammar and wording defects fixed

For more details, see the release notes.

Certified Tester Advanced Level
Test Analyst (CTAL-TA)

Table of Contents

Revision History 3
Table of Contents 4
Acknowledgments 6
0. Introduction to this Syllabus 8
   0.1 Purpose of this Syllabus 8
   0.2 The Certified Tester Advanced Level in Software Testing 8
   0.3 Examinable Learning Objectives and Cognitive Levels of Knowledge 8
   0.4 The Advanced Level Test Analyst Exam 9
   0.5 Entry Requirements for the Exam 9
   0.6 Expectations of Experience 9
   0.7 Accreditation of Courses 9
   0.8 Level of Syllabus Detail 9
   0.9 How this Syllabus is Organized 10
1.   The Test Analyst's Tasks in the Test Process - 150 mins 11
   1.1 Introduction 12
   1.2 Testing in the Software Development Lifecycle 12
   1.3 Test Analysis 13
   1.4 Test Design 14
      1.4.1 Low-level and High-level Test Cases 15
      1.4.2 Design of Test Cases 16
   1.5 Test Implementation 17
   1.6 Test Execution 19
2.   The Test Analyst's Tasks in Risk-Based Testing - 60 mins 20
   2.1 Introduction 21
   2.2 Risk Identification 21
   2.3 Risk Assessment 21
   2.4 Risk Mitigation 22
      2.4.1 Prioritizing the Tests 23
      2.4.2 Adjusting Testing for Future Test Cycles 23
3.   Test Techniques - 630 mins 24
   3.1 Introduction 25
   3.2 Black-Box Test Techniques 25
      3.2.1 Equivalence Partitioning 25
      3.2.2 Boundary Value Analysis 27
      3.2.3 Decision Table Testing 28
      3.2.4 State Transition Testing 29
      3.2.5 Classification Tree Technique 31
      3.2.6 Pairwise Testing 32
      3.2.7 Use Case Testing 33
      3.2.8 Combining Techniques 34
   3.3 Experience-Based Test Techniques 34
      3.3.1 Error Guessing 35
      3.3.2 Checklist-Based Testing 36
      3.3.3 Exploratory Testing 37
      3.3.4 Defect-Based Test Techniques 38
   3.4 Applying the Most Appropriate Technique 39
4.   Testing Software Quality Characteristics - 180 mins 40
   4.1 Introduction 41
   4.2 Quality Characteristics for Business Domain Testing 42
      4.2.1 Functional Correctness Testing 42

	4.2.2 Functional Appropriateness Testing	42
	4.2.3 Functional Completeness Testing	42
	4.2.4 Interoperability Testing	43
	4.2.5 Usability Evaluation	43
	4.2.6 Portability Testing	45
5.	Reviews - 120 mins	47
	5.1 Introduction	48
	5.2 Using Checklists in Reviews	48
	5.2.1 Requirements Reviews	48
	5.2.2 User Story Reviews	49
	5.2.3 Tailoring Checklists	49
6.	Test Tools and Automation - 90 mins	51
	6.1 Introduction	52
	6.2 Keyword-Driven Testing	52
	6.3 Types of Test Tools	53
	6.3.1 Test Design Tools	53
	6.3.2 Test Data Preparation Tools	53
	6.3.3 Automated Test Execution Tools	53
7.	References	55
	7.1 Standards	55
	7.2 ISTQB® and IREB Documents	55
	7.3 Books and Articles	55
	7.4 Other References	57
8.	Appendix A	58
9.	Index	59

Acknowledgments

This document was produced by the Test Analyst task force of the International Software Testing Qualifications Board Advanced Level Working Group: Mette Bruhn-Pedersen (Working Group Chair); Matthias Hamburg (Product Owner); Wim Decoutere, István Forgács, Adam Roman, Jan Sabak, Marc-Florian Wendland (Authors).

The task force thanks Paul Weymouth and Richard Green for their technical editing, Gary Mogyorodi for the Glossary conformance checks, and the Member Boards for their review comments related to the published 2019 version of the Syllabus and the proposed changes.

The following persons participated in the reviewing and commenting on this syllabus:
Gery Ágnecz, Armin Born, Chenyifan, Klaudia Dussa-Zieger, Chen Geng (Kevin), Istvan Gercsák, Richard Green, Ole Chr. Hansen, Zsolt Hargitai, Andreas Hetz, Tobias Horn, Joan Killeen, Attila Kovacs, Rik Marselis, Marton Matyas, Blair Mo, Gary Mogyorodi, Ingvar Nordström, Tal Pe'er, Palma Polyak, Nishan Portoyan, Meile Posthuma, Stuart Reid, Murian Song, Péter Sótér, Lucjan Stapp, Benjamin Timmermans, Chris van Bael, Stephanie van Dijck, Paul Weymouth.

This document was released by ISTQB® on 23.Feb.2021

Subsequently, formal, grammar and wording improvements have been suggested by Tal Pe'er, Stuart Reid, Marc-Florian Wendland and Matthias Hamburg which have been implemented and published in the Errata 3.1.1 and 3.1.2.

The version 2019 of this document was produced by a core team from the International Software Testing Qualifications Board Advanced Level Working Group: Graham Bath, Judy McKay, Mike Smith

The following persons participated in the reviewing, commenting, and balloting of the 2019 version of this syllabus:
Laura Albert, Markus Beck, Henriett Braunné Bokor, Francisca Cano Ortiz, Guo Chaonian, Wim Decoutere, Milena Donato, Klaudia Dussa-Zieger, Melinda Eckrich-Brajer, Péter Földházi Jr, David Frei, Chen Geng, Matthias Hamburg, Zsolt Hargitai, Zhai Hongbao, Tobias Horn, Ágota Horváth, Beata Karpinska, Attila Kovács, József Kreisz, Dietrich Leimsner, Ren Liang, Claire Lohr, Ramit Manohar Kaul, Rik Marselis, Marton Matyas, Don Mills, Blair Mo, Gary Mogyorodi, Ingvar Nordström, Tal Peer, Pálma Polyák, Meile Posthuma, Lloyd Roden, Adam Roman, Abhishek Sharma, Péter Sótér, Lucjan Stapp, Andrea Szabó, Jan te Kock, Benjamin Timmermans, Chris Van Bael, Erik van Veenendaal, Jan Versmissen, Carsten Weise, Robert Werkhoven, Paul Weymouth.

The version 2012 of this document was produced by a core team from the International Software Testing Qualifications Board Advanced Level Sub Working Group - Advanced Test Analyst: Judy McKay (Chair), Mike Smith, Erik van Veenendaal.

At the time the Advanced Level Syllabus was completed the Advanced Level Working Group had the following membership (alphabetical order):
Graham Bath, Rex Black, Maria Clara Choucair, Debra Friedenberg, Bernard Homès (Vice Chair), Paul Jorgensen, Judy McKay, Jamie Mitchell, Thomas Mueller, Klaus Olsen, Kenji Onishi, Meile Posthuma, Eric Riou du Cosquer, Jan Sabak, Hans Schaefer, Mike Smith (Chair), Geoff Thompson, Erik van Veenendaal, Tsuyoshi Yumoto.

The following persons participated in the reviewing, commenting and balloting of the 2012 version of the syllabus:
Graham Bath, Arne Becher, Rex Black, Piet de Roo, Frans Dijkman, Mats Grindal, Kobi Halperin, Bernard Homès, Maria Jönsson, Junfei Ma, Eli Margolin, Rik Marselis, Don Mills, Gary Mogyorodi,

Stefan Mohacsi, Reto Mueller, Thomas Mueller, Ingvar Nordstrom, Tal Pe'er, Raluca Madalina Popescu, Stuart Reid, Jan Sabak, Hans Schaefer, Marco Sogliani, Yaron Tsubery, Hans Weiberg, Paul Weymouth, Chris van Bael, Jurian van der Laar, Stephanie van Dijk, Erik van Veenendaal, Wenqiang Zheng, Debi Zylbermann.

0. Introduction to this Syllabus

0.1 Purpose of this Syllabus

This syllabus forms the basis for the International Software Testing Qualification at the Advanced Level for the Test Analyst. The ISTQB® provides this syllabus as follows:

1. To National Boards, to translate into their local language and to accredit training providers. National Boards may adapt the syllabus to their particular language needs and modify the references to adapt to their local publications.
2. To Exam Boards, to derive examination questions in their local language adapted to the learning objectives for each syllabus.
3. To training providers, to produce courseware and determine appropriate teaching methods.
4. To certification candidates, to prepare for the exam (as part of a training course or independently).
5. To the international software and systems engineering community, to advance the profession of software and systems testing, and as a basis for books and articles.

The ISTQB® may allow other entities to use this syllabus for other purposes, provided they seek and obtain prior written permission.

0.2 The Certified Tester Advanced Level in Software Testing

The Advanced Level Core qualification is comprised of three separate syllabi relating to the following roles:
- Test Manager
- Test Analyst
- Technical Test Analyst

The ISTQB® Advanced Level Overview 2019 is a separate document [ISTQB_AL_OVIEW] which includes the following information:
- Business Outcomes for each syllabus
- Matrix showing traceability between business outcomes and learning objectives
- Summary for each syllabus
- Relationships between the syllabi

0.3 Examinable Learning Objectives and Cognitive Levels of Knowledge

The Learning Objectives support the Business Outcomes and are used to create the examination for achieving the Advanced Test Analyst Certification.

The knowledge levels of the specific learning objectives at K2, K3 and K4 levels are shown at the beginning of each chapter and are classified as follows:
- K2: Understand
- K3: Apply
- K4: Analyze

The definitions of all terms listed as keywords just below the chapter headings shall be remembered (K1), even if not explicitly mentioned in the learning objectives.

Certified Tester Advanced Level
Test Analyst (CTAL-TA)

0.4 The Advanced Level Test Analyst Exam

The Advanced Level Test Analyst exam will be based on this syllabus. Answers to exam questions may require the use of materials based on more than one section of this syllabus. All sections of the syllabus are examinable except for the introduction and the appendices. Standards, books and other ISTQB® syllabi are included as references, but their content is not examinable beyond what is summarized in this syllabus itself from such standards, books and other ISTQB® syllabi.

The format of the exam is multiple choice. There are 40 questions. To pass the exam, at least 65% of the total points must be earned.

Exams may be taken as part of an accredited training course or taken independently (e.g., at an exam center or in a public exam). Completion of an accredited training course is not a pre-requisite for the exam.

0.5 Entry Requirements for the Exam

The Certified Tester Foundation Level certificate shall be obtained before taking the Advanced Level Test Analyst certification exam.

0.6 Expectations of Experience

None of the learning objectives for the Advanced Test Analyst assume that specific experience is available.

0.7 Accreditation of Courses

An ISTQB® Member Board may accredit training providers whose course material follows this syllabus. Training providers should obtain accreditation guidelines from the Member Board or body that performs the accreditation. An accredited course is recognized as conforming to this syllabus, and is allowed to have an ISTQB® exam as part of the course.

0.8 Level of Syllabus Detail

The level of detail in this syllabus allows internationally consistent courses and exams. In order to achieve this goal, the syllabus consists of:

- General instructional objectives describing the intention of the Advanced Level Test Analyst
- A list of items that students must be able to recall
- Learning objectives of each knowledge area, describing the cognitive learning outcome to be achieved
- A description of the key concepts, including references to sources such as accepted literature or standards

The syllabus content is not a description of the entire knowledge area; it reflects the level of detail to be covered in Advanced Level training courses. It focuses on material that can apply to all software projects, including Agile software development. The syllabus does not contain any specific learning objectives relating to any particular software development lifecycle (SDLC), but it does discuss how these concepts apply in Agile software development, other types of iterative and incremental lifecycles, and in sequential lifecycles.

0.9 How this Syllabus is Organized

There are six chapters with examinable content. The top-level heading of each chapter specifies the minimum time for instruction and exercises for the chapter; timing is not provided below the chapter level. For accredited training courses, the syllabus requires a minimum of 20 hours and 30 minutes of instruction, distributed across the six chapters as follows:

- Chapter 1: The Test Analyst's Tasks in the Test Process (150 minutes)
- Chapter 2: The Test Analyst's Tasks in Risk-Based Testing (60 minutes)
- Chapter 3: Test Techniques (630 minutes)
- Chapter 4: Testing Software Quality Characteristics (180 minutes)
- Chapter 5: Reviews (120 minutes)
- Chapter 6: Test Tools and Automation (90 minutes)

1. The Test Analyst's Tasks in the Test Process - 150 mins.

Keywords
exit criteria, high-level test case, low-level test case, test, test analysis, test basis, test condition, test data, test design, test execution, test execution schedule, test implementation, test procedure, test suite

Learning Objectives for the Test Analyst's Tasks in the Test Process

1.1 Introduction
No learning objectives

1.2 Testing in the Software Development Lifecycle
TA-1.2.1　(K2) Explain how and why the timing and level of involvement for the Test Analyst varies when working with different software development lifecycle models

1.3 Test Analysis
TA-1.3.1　(K2) Summarize the appropriate tasks for the Test Analyst when conducting analysis activities

1.4 Test Design
TA-1.4.1　(K2) Explain why test conditions should be understood by the stakeholders
TA-1.4.2　(K4) For a given project scenario, select the appropriate design level for test cases (high-level or low-level)
TA-1.4.3　(K2) Explain the issues to be considered in test case design

1.5 Test Implementation
TA-1.5.1　(K2) Summarize the appropriate tasks for the Test Analyst when conducting test implementation activities

1.6 Test Execution
TA-1.6.1　(K2) Summarize the appropriate tasks for the Test Analyst when conducting test execution activities

1.1 Introduction

In the ISTQB® Foundation Level syllabus, the test process is described as including the following activities:
- Test planning
- Test monitoring and control
- Test analysis
- Test design
- Test implementation
- Test execution
- Test completion

In this Advanced Level Test Analyst syllabus, the activities which have particular relevance for the Test Analyst are considered in more depth. This provides additional refinement of the test process to better fit different software development lifecycle (SDLC) models.

Determining the appropriate tests, designing and implementing them and then executing them are the primary areas of concentration for the Test Analyst. While it is important to understand the other steps in the test process, the majority of the Test Analyst's work usually focuses on the following activities:
- Test analysis
- Test design
- Test implementation
- Test execution

The other activities of the test process are adequately described at the Foundation Level and do not need further elaboration at this level.

1.2 Testing in the Software Development Lifecycle

The overall SDLC should be considered when defining a test strategy. The moment of involvement for the Test Analyst is different for the various SDLCs; the amount of involvement, time required, information available and expectations can be quite varied as well. The Test Analyst must be aware of the types of information to supply to other related organizational roles such as:
- Requirements engineering and management - requirements reviews feedback
- Project management - schedule input
- Configuration and change management – results of build verification testing, version control information
- Software development - notifications of defects found
- Software maintenance - reports on defects, defect removal efficiency, and confirmation testing
- Technical support - accurate documentation for workarounds and known issues
- Production of technical documentation (e.g., database design specifications, test environment documentation) - input to these documents as well as technical review of the documents

Test activities must be aligned with the chosen SDLC whose nature may be sequential, iterative, incremental, or a hybrid of these. For example, in the sequential V-model, the test process applied to the system test level could align as follows:
- System test planning occurs concurrently with project planning, and test monitoring and control continues until test completion. This will influence the schedule inputs provided by the Test Analyst for project management purposes.

- System test analysis and design aligns with documents such as the system requirements specification, system and architectural (high-level) design specification, and component (low-level) design specification.
- Implementation of the system test environment might start during system design, though the bulk of it typically would occur concurrently with coding and component testing, with work on system test implementation activities stretching often until just days before the start of system test execution.
- System test execution begins when the entry criteria are met or, if necessary, waived, which typically means that at least component testing and often also component integration testing have met their exit criteria. System test execution continues until the system test exit criteria are met.
- System test completion activities occur after the system test exit criteria are met.

Iterative and incremental models may not follow the same order of activities and may exclude some activities. For example, an iterative model may utilize a reduced set of test activities for each iteration. Test analysis, design, implementation, and execution may be conducted for each iteration, whereas high-level planning is done at the beginning of the project, and completion tasks are done at the end.

In Agile software development, it is common to use a less formalized process and a much closer working relationship with project stakeholders that allows changes to occur more easily within the project. There may not be a well-defined Test Analyst role. There is less comprehensive test documentation, and communication is shorter and more frequent.

Agile software development involves testing from the outset. This starts from the initiation of the product development as the developers perform their initial architecture and design work. Reviews may not be formalized but are continuous as the software evolves. Involvement is expected to be throughout the project and Test Analyst tasks are expected to be done by the team.

Iterative and incremental models range from Agile software development, where there is an expectation for change as the customer requirements evolve, to hybrid models, e.g., iterative/incremental development combined with a V-model approach. In such hybrid models, Test Analysts should be involved in the planning and design aspects of the sequential activities, and then move to a more interactive role during the iterative/incremental activities.

Whatever the SDLC being used, Test Analysts need to understand the expectations for involvement as well as the timing of that involvement. Test Analysts provide an effective contribution to software quality by adjusting their activities and their moment of involvement to the specific SDLC rather than sticking to a pre-defined role model.

1.3 Test Analysis

During test planning, the scope of the testing project is defined. During test analysis, Test Analysts use this scope definition to:
- Analyze the test basis
- Identify defects of various types in the test basis
- Identify and prioritize test conditions and features to be tested
- Capture bi-directional traceability between each element of the test basis and the associated test conditions
- Perform tasks associated with risk-based testing (see Chapter 2)

In order for Test Analysts to proceed effectively with test analysis, the following entry criteria should be met:

- There is a body of knowledge (e.g., requirements, user stories) describing the test object that can serve as its test basis (see [ISTQB_FL_SYL] Sections 1.4.2 and 2.2 or a list of other possible sources of test basis).
- This test basis has passed review with reasonable results and has been updated as needed after the review. Note that if high-level test cases are to be defined (see Section 1.4.1), the test basis may not yet need to be fully defined. In Agile software development, this review cycle will be iterative as the user stories are refined at the beginning of each iteration.
- There is an approved budget and schedule available to accomplish the remaining testing tasks for this test object.

Test conditions are typically identified by analysis of the test basis in conjunction with the test objectives (as defined in test planning). In some situations, where documentation may be old or non-existent, the test conditions may be identified by discussion with relevant stakeholders (e.g., in workshops or during iteration planning). In Agile software development, the acceptance criteria, which are defined as part of user stories, are often used as the basis for the test design.

While test conditions are usually specific to the item being tested, there are some standard considerations for the Test Analyst.
- It is usually advisable to define test conditions at differing levels of detail. Initially, high-level conditions are identified to define general targets for testing, such as "functionality of screen x". Subsequently, more detailed conditions are identified as the basis of specific test cases, such as "screen x rejects an account number that is one digit short of the correct length". Using this type of hierarchical approach to defining test conditions can help to ensure the coverage is sufficient for the high-level items. This approach also allows a Test Analyst to start working on defining high-level test conditions for user stories that have not yet been refined.
- If product risks have been defined, then the test conditions that will be necessary to address each product risk should be identified and traced back to that risk item.

The application of test techniques (as identified within the test strategy and/or the test plan) can be helpful in test analysis activities and may be used to support the following objectives:
- Identifying test conditions
- Reducing the likelihood of omitting important test conditions
- Defining more precise and accurate test conditions

After the test conditions have been identified and refined, review of these conditions with the stakeholders can be conducted to ensure the requirements are clearly understood and that testing is aligned with the goals of the project.

At the conclusion of the test analysis activities for a given area (e.g., a specific function), the Test Analyst should know what specific tests must be designed for that area.

1.4 Test Design

Still adhering to the scope determined during test planning, the test process continues as the Test Analyst designs the tests which will be implemented and executed. Test design includes the following activities:
- Determining in which test areas low-level or high-level test cases are appropriate
- Determining the test technique(s) that will enable the necessary coverage to be achieved. The techniques that may be used are established during test planning.
- Using test techniques to design test cases and sets of test cases that cover the identified test conditions
- Identifying necessary test data to support test conditions and test cases
- Designing the test environment and identifying any required infrastructure including tools

- Capturing bi-directional traceability (e.g., between the test basis, test conditions and test cases)

Prioritization criteria identified during risk analysis and test planning should be applied throughout the process, from analysis and design to implementation and execution.

Depending on the types of tests being designed, one of the entry criteria for test design may be the availability of tools that will be used during the design work.

During test design, the Test Analyst must consider at least the following:
- Some test items are better addressed by defining only the test conditions rather than going further into the definition of test scripts, which give the sequence of instructions required to execute a test. In this case, the test conditions should be defined to be used as a guide for unscripted testing.
- The pass/fail criteria should be clearly identified.
- Tests should be designed to be understandable by other testers, not just the author. If the author is not the person who executes the test, other testers will need to read and understand previously specified tests in order to understand the test objectives and the relative importance of the test.
- Tests must also be understandable for other stakeholders such as developers (who may review the tests) and auditors (who may have to approve the tests).
- Tests should cover all types of interaction with the test object and should not be restricted to the interactions of people through the user-visible interface. They may also include, for example, interaction with other systems and technical or physical events. (see [IREB_CPRE] for further details).
- Tests should be designed to test the interfaces between the various test items, as well as the behaviors of the items themselves.
- Test design effort must be prioritized and balanced to align with the risk levels and business value.

1.4.1 Low-level and High-level Test Cases

One of the jobs of the Test Analyst is to determine the best design level of test cases for a given situation. Low-level and high-level test cases are covered in [ISTQB_FL_SYL]. Some of the advantages and disadvantages of using these are described in the following lists:

Low-level test cases provide the following advantages:
- Inexperienced testing staff can rely on detailed information provided within the project. Low-level test cases provide all the specific information and procedures needed for the tester to execute the test case (including any data requirements) and to verify the actual results.
- Tests may be rerun by different testers and should achieve the same test results.
- Non-obvious defects in the test basis can be revealed.
- The level of detail enables an independent verification of the tests, such as audits, if required.
- Time spent on automated test case implementation can be reduced.

Low-level test cases have the following disadvantages:
- They may require a significant amount of effort, both for creation and maintenance.
- They tend to limit tester ingenuity during execution.
- They require that the test basis be well defined.
- Their traceability to test conditions may take more effort than with high-level test cases.

High-level test cases provide the following advantages:
- They give guidelines for what should be tested, and allow the Test Analyst to vary the actual data or even the procedure that is followed when executing the test.
- They may provide better risk coverage than low-level test cases because they will vary somewhat each time they are executed.
- They can be defined early in the requirements process.
- They make use of the Test Analyst's experience with both testing and the test object when the test is executed.
- They can be defined when no detailed and formal documentation is required.
- They are better suited for reuse in different test cycles when different test data can be used.

High-level test cases have the following disadvantages:
- They are less reproducible, making verification difficult. This is because they lack the detailed description found in low-level test cases.
- More experienced testing staff may be needed to execute them
- When automating on the basis of high-level test cases, the lack of details may result in validating the wrong actual results or missing items that should be validated.

High-level test cases may be used to develop low-level test cases when the requirements become more defined and stable. In this case, the test case creation is done sequentially, flowing from high-level to low-level with only the low-level test cases being used for execution.

1.4.2 Design of Test Cases

Test cases are designed by the stepwise elaboration and refinement of the identified test conditions using test techniques (see Chapter 3). Test cases should be repeatable, verifiable and traceable back to the test basis (e.g., requirements).

Test design includes the identification of the following:
- Objective (i.e., the observable, measurable objective of test execution)
- Preconditions, such as either project or localized test environment requirements and the plans for their delivery, state of the system prior to test execution, etc.
- Test data requirements (both input data for the test case as well as data that must exist in the system for the test case to be executed)
- Expected results with explicit pass/fail criteria
- Postconditions, such as affected data, state of the system after test execution, triggers for subsequent processing, etc.

A particular challenge can be the definition of the expected result of a test. Computing this manually is often tedious and error-prone; if possible, it might be preferable to find or create an automated test oracle. In identifying the expected result, testers are concerned not only with outputs on the screen, but also with data and environmental postconditions. If the test basis is clearly defined, identifying the correct result, theoretically, should be simple. However, test basis documentation might be vague, contradictory, lacking coverage of key areas, or missing entirely. In such cases, a Test Analyst must have subject matter expertise or have access to it. Also, even when the test basis is well specified, complex interactions of complex stimuli and responses can make the definition of the expected results difficult; therefore, a test oracle is essential. In Agile software development, the test oracle might be the product owner. Test case execution without any way to determine correctness of actual results might have a very low added value or benefit, often generating invalid test reports or false confidence in the system.

The activities described above may be applied to all test levels, though the test basis will vary. When analyzing and designing tests, it is important to remember the target level for the test as well as the objective of the test. This helps to determine the level of detail required as well as any tools that may be needed (e.g., drivers and stubs at the component test level).

During the development of test conditions and test cases, some amount of documentation is typically created, resulting in test work products. In practice the extent to which test work products are documented varies considerably. This can be affected by any of the following:
- Project risks (what must/must not be documented)
- The added value which the documentation brings to the project
- Standards to be followed and/or regulations to be met
- SDLC or approach used (e.g., an Agile approach aims for "just enough" documentation)
- The requirement for traceability from the test basis through test analysis and design

Depending on the scope of the testing, test analysis and design address the quality characteristics for the test object(s). The ISO 25010 standard [ISO25010] provides a useful reference. When testing hardware/software systems, additional characteristics may apply.

The activities of test analysis and test design may be enhanced by intertwining them with reviews and static analysis. In fact, conducting the test analysis and test design are often a form of static testing because problems may be found in the test basis documents during this activity. Test analysis and test design based on the requirements specification is an excellent way to prepare for a requirements review meeting. Reading the requirements to use them for creating tests requires understanding the requirement and being able to determine a way to assess fulfillment of the requirement. This activity often uncovers missing requirements, requirements that are not clear, are untestable, or do not have defined acceptance criteria. Similarly, test work products such as test cases, risk analyses, and test plans can be subjected to reviews.

If testing requires infrastructure that is not readily available, the Test Analyst should define the detailed test infrastructure requirements during test design. Should these requirements not be completed in time, test implementation will be at risk of overrun due to unexpected time and effort. It must be remembered that test infrastructure includes more than test objects and testware. For example the infrastructure requirements may include rooms, equipment, personnel, software, tools, peripherals, communications equipment, user authorizations, and all other items required to run the tests.

The exit criteria for test analysis and test design will vary depending on the project parameters, but all items discussed in these two sections should be considered for inclusion in the defined exit criteria. It is important that the exit criteria are measurable and that all the information required for the subsequent steps has been provided and all necessary preparation has been performed.

1.5 Test Implementation

Test implementation prepares the testware needed for test execution based on test analysis and design. It includes the following activities:
- Developing test procedures, and, potentially, creating automated test scripts
- Organizing test procedures and automated test scripts (if there are any) into test suites to be executed in a specific test run
- Consulting the Test Manager in prioritizing the test cases and test suites to be executed
- Creating a test execution schedule, including resource allocation, to enable test execution to begin (see [ISTQB_FL_SYL] Section 5.2.4)
- Finalizing preparation of test data and test environments

- Updating the traceability between the test basis and testware such as test conditions, test cases, test procedures, test scripts and test suites.

During test implementation, Test Analysts identify an efficient execution order of test cases and create test procedures. Defining the test procedures requires carefully identifying constraints and dependencies that might influence the test execution sequence. Test procedures document any initial preconditions (e.g., loading of test data from a data repository) and any activities following execution (e.g., resetting the system status).

Test Analysts identify test procedures and automated test scripts that can be grouped (e.g., they all relate to the testing of a particular high-level business process), and organize them into test suites. This enables related test cases to be executed together.

Test Analysts arrange test suites within a test execution schedule in a way that results in efficient test execution. If a risk-based test strategy is being used, the risk level will be the primary consideration in determining the execution order for the test cases. There may be other factors that determine test case execution order such as the availability of the right people, equipment, data and the functionality to be tested.

It is not unusual for code to be released in sections and the test effort has to be coordinated with the sequence in which the software becomes available for testing. Particularly in iterative and incremental development models, it is important for the Test Analyst to coordinate with the development team to ensure that the software will be released for testing in a testable order.

The level of detail and associated complexity for work done during test implementation may be influenced by the detail of the test conditions and test cases. In some cases regulatory rules apply, and test work products should provide evidence of compliance to applicable standards such as the United States standard DO-178C (in Europe, ED 12C). [RTCA DO-178C/ED-12C].

As specified above, test data is needed for most testing, and in some cases these sets of data can be quite large. During implementation, Test Analysts create input and environment data to load into databases and other such repositories. This data must be "fit for purpose" to enable detection of defects. Test Analysts may also create data to be used with data-driven and keyword-driven testing (see Section 6.2) as well as for manual testing.

Test implementation is also concerned with the test environment(s). During this activity the environment(s) should be fully set up and verified prior to test execution. A "fit for purpose" test environment is essential, i.e., the test environment should be capable of enabling the exposure of the defects present during controlled testing, operate normally when failures are not occurring, and adequately replicate, if required, the production or end-user environment for higher test levels. Test environment changes may be necessary during test execution depending on unanticipated changes, test results or other considerations. If environment changes do occur during execution, it is important to assess the impact of the changes to tests that have already been run.

During test implementation, Test Analysts should check that those responsible for the creation and maintenance of the test environment are known and available, and that all the testware and test support tools and associated processes are ready for use. This includes configuration management, defect management, and test logging and management. In addition, Test Analysts must verify the procedures that gather data for evaluating current status against exit criteria and test results reporting.

It is wise to use a balanced approach to test implementation as determined during test planning. For example, risk-based analytical test strategies are often blended with reactive test strategies. In this case, some percentage of the test implementation effort is allocated to testing which does not follow predetermined scripts (unscripted).

Unscripted testing should not be random or aimless as this can be unpredictable in duration and coverage, and give a low yield in defects. Rather, it should be conducted in time boxed sessions, each given initial direction by a test charter, but with the freedom to depart from the charter's prescriptions if potentially more productive test opportunities are discovered in the course of the session. Over the years, testers have developed a variety of experience-based test techniques, such as attacks [Whittaker03], error guessing [Myers11], and exploratory testing [Whittaker09]. Test analysis, test design, and test implementation still occur, but they take place primarily during test execution.

When following such reactive test strategies, the results of each test influence the analysis, design, and implementation of the subsequent tests. While these strategies are lightweight and often effective at finding defects, there are some drawbacks, including the following:
- Expertise from the Test Analyst is required
- Duration can be difficult to predict
- Coverage can be difficult to track
- Repeatability can be lost without good documentation or tool support

1.6 Test Execution

Test execution is conducted according to the test execution schedule and includes the following tasks: (see [ISTQB_FL_SYL])
- Executing manual tests, including exploratory testing
- Executing automated tests
- Comparing actual results with expected results
- Analyzing anomalies to establish their likely causes
- Reporting defects based on the failures observed
- Logging the actual results of test execution
- Updating the traceability between the test basis and testware to consider test results
- Executing regression tests

The test execution tasks listed above may be conducted by either the tester or the Test Analyst. The

following are typical additional tasks which may be performed by the Test Analyst:
- Recognizing defect clusters which may indicate the need for more testing of a particular part of the test object
- Making suggestions for future exploratory testing sessions based on the findings from exploratory testing
- Identifying new risks from information obtained when performing test execution tasks
- Making suggestions for improving any of the work products from the test implementation activity (e.g., improvements to test procedures)

2. The Test Analyst's Tasks in Risk-Based Testing - 60 mins.

Keywords
product risk, risk identification, risk mitigation, risk-based testing

Learning Objectives for The Test Analyst's Tasks in Risk-Based Testing The

Test Analyst's Tasks in Risk-Based Testing
TA-2.1.1   (K3) For a given situation, participate in risk identification, perform risk assessment and propose appropriate risk mitigation

2.1 Introduction

Test Managers often have overall responsibility for establishing and managing a risk-based test strategy. They will usually request the involvement of a Test Analyst to ensure the risk-based approach is implemented correctly.

Test Analysts should be actively involved in the following risk-based testing tasks:
- Risk identification
- Risk assessment
- Risk mitigation

These tasks are performed iteratively throughout the SDLC to deal with emerging risks, changing priorities and to regularly evaluate and communicate risk status (see [vanVeenendaal12] and [Black02] for further details). In Agile software development, the three tasks are often combined in a so-called risk session with focus on either an iteration or a release.

Test Analysts should work within the risk-based test framework established for the project by the Test Manager. They should contribute their knowledge of the business domain risks that are inherent in the project such as risks related to safety, business and economic concerns, and political factors, among others.

2.2 Risk Identification

By calling on the broadest possible sample of stakeholders, the risk identification process is most likely to detect the largest possible number of significant risks.

Test Analysts often possess unique knowledge regarding the particular business domain of the system under test. This means they are particularly well suited to the following tasks:
- Conducting expert interviews with the domain experts and users
- Conducting independent assessments
- Using risk templates
- Participating in risk workshops
- Participating in brainstorming sessions with potential and current users
- Defining testing checklists
- Calling on past experience with similar systems or projects

In particular, Test Analysts should work closely with the users and other domain experts (e.g., requirement engineers, business analysts) to determine the areas of business risk that should be addressed during testing. In Agile software development, this close relationship with stakeholders enables risk identification to be conducted on a regular basis, such as during iteration planning meetings.

Sample risks that might be identified in a project include:
- Issues with functional correctness, e.g., incorrect calculations
- Usability issues, e.g., insufficient keyboard shortcuts
- Portability issues, e.g., inability to install an application on particular platforms

2.3 Risk Assessment

While risk identification is about identifying as many pertinent risks as possible, risk assessment is the study of these identified risks. Specifically, categorizing each risk and determining its risk level.

Determining the risk level typically involves assessing, for each risk item, the risk likelihood and the risk impact. The risk likelihood is usually interpreted as the likelihood that the potential problem can exist in the system under test and will be observed when the system is in production. Technical Test Analysts should contribute to finding and understanding the potential likelihood for each risk item whereas Test Analysts contribute to understanding the potential business impact of the problem should it occur (in Agile software development this role-based distinction may be less strong).

The risk impact is often interpreted as the severity of the effect on the users, customers, or other stakeholders. In other words, it arises from business risk. Test Analysts should contribute to identifying and assessing the potential business domain or user impact for each risk item. Factors influencing business risk include the following:
- Frequency of use of the affected feature
- Business loss
- Financial damage
- Ecological or social losses or liability
- Civil or criminal legal sanctions
- Safety concerns
- Fines, loss of license
- Lack of reasonable workarounds if people cannot work any more
- Visibility of the feature
- Visibility of failure leading to negative publicity and potential image damage
- Loss of customers

Given the available risk information, Test Analysts need to establish the levels of business risk according to the guidelines provided by a Test Manager. These could be classified using an ordinal scale (actual numeric or low/medium/high), or traffic signal colors. Once the risk likelihood and risk impact have been assigned, Test Managers use these values to determine the risk level for each risk item. That risk level is then used to prioritize the risk mitigation activities.[vanVeenendaal12].

2.4 Risk Mitigation

During the project, Test Analysts should seek to do the following:
- Reduce product risk by designing effective test cases that demonstrate unambiguously whether tests pass or fail, and by participating in reviews of software work products such as requirements, designs, and user documentation
- Implement appropriate risk mitigation activities identified in the test strategy and test plan (e.g., test a particularly high risk business process using particular test techniques)
- Re-evaluate known risks based on additional information gathered as the project unfolds, adjusting risk likelihood, risk impact, or both, as appropriate
- Identify new risks from information obtained during testing

When one is talking about a product risk, then testing makes an essential contribution to mitigating such risks. By finding defects, testers reduce risk by providing awareness of the defects and opportunities to deal with the defects before release. If the testers find no defects, testing then reduces risk by providing evidence that, under certain conditions (i.e., the conditions tested), the system operates correctly. Test Analysts help to determine risk mitigation options by investigating opportunities for gathering accurate test data, creating and testing realistic user scenarios and conducting or overseeing usability studies, among others.

2.4.1 Prioritizing the Tests

The level of risk is also used to prioritize tests. A Test Analyst might determine that there is a high risk in the area of transactional accuracy in an accounting system. As a result, to mitigate the risk, the tester may work with other business domain experts to gather a strong set of sample data that can be processed and verified for accuracy. Similarly, a Test Analyst might determine that usability issues are a significant risk for a new test object. Rather than wait for a user acceptance test to discover any issues, the Test Analyst might prioritize an early usability test based on a prototype to help identify and resolve usability design problems early before the user acceptance test. This prioritization must be considered as early as possible in the planning stages so that the schedule can accommodate the necessary testing at the necessary time.

In some cases, all of the highest risk tests are run before any lower-risk tests, and tests are run in strict risk order (called "depth-first"); in other cases, a sampling approach is used to select a sample of tests across all the identified risk areas using risk level to weight the selection while at the same time ensuring coverage of every risk at least once (called "breadth-first").

Whether risk-based testing proceeds depth-first or breadth-first, it is possible that the time allocated for testing might be consumed without all tests being run. Risk-based testing allows testers to report to management in terms of the remaining level of risk at this point, and allows management to decide whether to extend testing or to transfer the remaining risk onto the users, customers, help desk/technical support, and/or operational staff.

2.4.2 Adjusting Testing for Future Test Cycles

Risk assessment is not a one-time activity performed before the start of test implementation; it is a continuous process. Each future planned test cycle should be subjected to new risk analysis to take into account such factors as:
- Any new or significantly changed product risks
- Unstable or failure-prone areas discovered during the testing
- Risks from fixed defects
- Typical defects found during testing
- Under-tested areas (low requirements coverage)

3. Test Techniques - 630 mins.

Keywords
black-box test technique, boundary value analysis, checklist-based testing, classification tree technique, decision table testing, defect taxonomy, defect-based test technique, equivalence partitioning, error guessing, experience-based testing, experience-based test technique, exploratory testing, pairwise testing, state transition testing, test charter, use case testing

Learning Objectives for Test Techniques

3.1 Introduction
No learning objectives

3.2 Black-Box Test Techniques
TA-3.2.1 (K4) Analyze a given specification item(s) and design test cases by applying equivalence partitioning
TA-3.2.2 (K4) Analyze a given specification item(s) and design test cases by applying boundary value analysis
TA-3.2.3 (K4) Analyze a given specification item(s) and design test cases by applying decision table testing
TA-3.2.4 (K4) Analyze a given specification item(s) and design test cases by applying state transition testing
TA-3.2.5 (K2) Explain how classification tree diagrams support test techniques
TA-3.2.6 (K4) Analyze a given specification item(s) and design test cases by applying pairwise testing
TA-3.2.7 (K4) Analyze a given specification item(s) and design test cases by applying use case testing
TA-3.2.8 (K4) Analyze a system, or its requirement specification, in order to determine likely types of defects to be found and select the appropriate black-box test technique(s)

3.3 Experience-Based Test Techniques
TA-3.3.1 (K2) Explain the principles of experience-based test techniques and the benefits and drawbacks compared to black-box and defect-based test techniques
TA-3.3.2 (K3) Identify exploratory tests from a given scenario
TA-3.3.3 (K2) Describe the application of defect-based test techniques and differentiate their use from black-box test techniques

3.4 Applying the Most Appropriate Test Techniques
TA-3.4.1 (K4) For a given project situation, determine which black-box or experience-based test techniques should be applied to achieve specific goals

3.1 Introduction

The test techniques considered in this chapter are divided into the following categories:
- Black-box
- Experience-based

These techniques are complementary and may be used as appropriate for any given test activity, regardless of which test level is being performed.

Note that both categories of techniques can be used to test functional and non-functional quality characteristics. Testing software characteristics is discussed in the next chapter.

The test techniques discussed in these sections may focus primarily on determining optimal test data (e.g., from equivalence partitions) or deriving test procedures (e.g., from state models). It is common to combine techniques to create complete test cases.

3.2 Black-Box Test Techniques

Black-box test techniques are introduced in the ISTQB® Foundation Level Syllabus [ISTQB_FL_SYL].

Common features of black-box test techniques include:
- Models, e.g., state transition diagrams and decision tables, are created during test design according to the test technique
- Test conditions are derived systematically from these models

Test techniques generally provide coverage criteria, which can be used for measuring test design and test execution activities. Completely fulfilling the coverage criteria does not mean that the entire set of tests is complete, but rather that the model no longer suggests any additional tests to increase coverage based on that technique.

Black-box testing is usually based on some form of specification documentation, such as a system requirement specification or user stories. Since the specification documentation should describe system behavior, particularly in the area of functionality, deriving tests from the requirements is often part of testing the behavior of the system. In some cases there may be no specification documentation but there are implied requirements, such as replacing the functionality of a legacy system.

There are a number of black-box test techniques. These techniques target different types of software and scenarios. The sections below show the applicability for each technique, some limitations and difficulties that the Test Analyst may experience, the method by which coverage is measured and the types of defects that are targeted.

Please refer to [ISO29119-4], [Bath14], [Beizer95], [Black07], [Black09], [Copeland04], [Craig02], [Forgács19], [Koomen06], and [Myers11] for further details.

3.2.1 Equivalence Partitioning

Equivalence partitioning (EP) is a technique used to reduce the number of test cases required to effectively test the handling of inputs, outputs, internal values and time-related values. Partitioning is used to create equivalence partitions (often called equivalence classes) which are created from sets of values that are required to be processed in the same manner. By selecting one representative value from a partition, coverage for all the items in the same partition is assumed.

Usually several parameters determine the behavior of the test object. When combining the equivalence partitions of different parameters into test cases, various techniques can be applied.

Applicability
This technique is applicable at any test level and is appropriate when all the members of a set of values to be tested are expected to be handled in the same way and where the sets of values used by the application do not interact. An equivalence partition can be any non-empty set of values, e.g.: ordered, unordered, discrete, continuous, infinite, finite, or even a singleton. The selection of sets of values is applicable to valid and invalid partitions (i.e., partitions containing values that should be considered invalid for the software under test).

EP is strongest when used in combination with boundary value analysis which expands the test values to include those on the edges of the partitions. EP, using values from the valid partitions, is a commonly used technique for smoke testing a new build or a new release as it quickly determines if basic functionality is working.

Limitations/Difficulties
If the assumption is incorrect and the values in the partition are not handled in exactly the same way, this technique may miss defects. It is also important to select the partitions carefully. For example, an input field that accepts positive and negative numbers might be better tested as two valid partitions, one for the positive numbers and one for the negative numbers, because of the likelihood of different handling. Depending on whether or not zero is allowed, this could become another partition. It is important for a Test Analyst to understand the underlying processing in order to determine the best partitioning of the values. This may require support in understanding code design.

The Test Analyst should also take into account possible dependencies between equivalence partitions of different parameters. For example, in a flight reservation system, the parameter "accompanying adult" may only be used in combination with the age class "child".

Coverage
Coverage is determined by taking the number of partitions for which a value has been tested and dividing that number by the number of partitions that have been identified. EP coverage is then stated as a percentage. Using multiple values for a single partition does not increase the coverage percentage.

If the behavior of the test object depends on a single parameter, each equivalence partition, whether valid or invalid, should be covered at least once.

In the case of more than one parameter, the Test Analyst should select a simple or combinatorial coverage type depending on the risk [Offutt16]. Differentiating between combinations containing only valid partitions and combinations containing one or more invalid partitions is therefore essential. Regarding the combinations with only valid equivalence partitions, the minimum requirement is a simple coverage of all valid partitions over all parameters. The minimum number of test cases needed in such a test suite equals the greatest number of valid partitions of a parameter, assuming the parameters are independent on each other. More thorough coverage types related to combinatorial techniques include the pairwise coverage (see Section 3.2.6 below), or the full coverage of any combination of valid partitions. Invalid equivalence partitions should be tested at least individually, i.e. in combination with valid partitions for the other parameters, in order to avoid defect masking. So each invalid partition contributes one test case to the test suite for simple coverage. In case of high risk, further combinations may be added to the test suite, e.g. consisting of only invalid partitions, or of pairs of invalid partitions.

Types of Defects
A Test Analyst uses this technique to find defects in the handling of various data values.

3.2.2 Boundary Value Analysis

Boundary value analysis (BVA) is used to test the proper handling of values that exist on the boundaries of ordered equivalence partitions. Two approaches to BVA are in common use: two-value boundary or three-value boundary testing. With two-value boundary testing, the boundary value (on the boundary) and the value that is just outside the boundary (by the smallest possible increment, based on the required accuracy) are used. For example, for amounts in a currency which has two decimal places, if the partition included the values from 1 to 10, the two-value test values for the upper boundary would be 10 and 10.01. The lower boundary test values would be 1 and 0.99. The boundaries are defined by the maximum and minimum values in the defined equivalence partition.

For three-value boundary testing, the values before, on and over the boundary are used. In the previous example, the upper boundary tests would include 9.99, 10 and 10.01. The lower boundary tests would include 0.99, 1 and 1.01. The decision regarding whether to use two-value or three-value boundary testing should be based on the risk associated with the item being tested, with the three-value boundary approach being used for the higher risk items.

Applicability
This technique is applicable at any test level and is appropriate when ordered equivalence partitions exist. For this reason the BVA technique is often conducted together with the EP technique. Ordered equivalence partitions are required because of the concept of being on and off the boundary. For example, a range of numbers is an ordered partition. A partition that consists of some text strings may be ordered too, e.g. by their lexicographic order, but if the ordering is not relevant from the business or technical point of view, then boundary values should not be in focus. In addition to number ranges, partitions for which boundary value analysis can be applied include:
- Numeric attributes of non-numeric variables (e.g., length)
- The number of loop execution cycles, including loops in state transition diagrams
- The number of iteration elements in stored data structures such as arrays
- The size of physical objects, e.g. memory
- The duration of activities

Limitations/Difficulties
Because the accuracy of this technique depends on the accurate identification of the equivalence partitions in order to correctly identify the boundaries, it is subject to the same limitations and difficulties as EP. The Test Analyst should also be aware of the precision in the valid and invalid values to be able to accurately determine the values to be tested. Only ordered partitions can be used for boundary value analysis but this is not limited to a range of valid inputs. For example, when testing for the number of cells supported by a spreadsheet, there is a partition that contains the number of cells up to and including the maximum allowed cells (the boundary) and another partition that begins with one cell over the maximum (over the boundary).

Coverage
Coverage is determined by taking the number of boundary conditions that are tested and dividing that by the number of identified boundary conditions (either using the two-value or three-value method). The coverage is stated as a percentage.
Similar to equivalence classes, in the case of multiple parameters, the Test Analyst should choose a simple or combinatorial coverage type, depending on the risk.

Types of Defects
Boundary value analysis reliably finds displacement or omission of boundaries, and may find cases of extra boundaries. This technique finds defects regarding the handling of the boundary values, particularly errors with less-than and greater-than logic (i.e., displacement). It can also be used to find non-functional defects, for example, a system supports 10,000 concurrent users but not 10,001.

3.2.3 Decision Table Testing

A decision table is a tabular representation of a set of conditions and related actions, expressed as rules indicating which action shall occur for which set of condition values [OMG-DMN]. Test Analysts can use decision tables to analyze the rules which apply to the software under test and design tests to cover those rules.

Conditions and the resulting actions of the test object form the rows of the decision table, usually with the conditions at the top and the actions at the bottom. The first column of the table contains the descriptions of the conditions and actions respectively. The following columns, called the rules, contain the condition values and corresponding action values respectively.

Decision tables in which conditions are Boolean with simple values "True" and "False" are called limited- entry decision tables. An example for such a condition is "User's income < 1000". Extended-entry decision tables allow for conditions having multiple values which may represent discrete elements or sets of elements. For example, a condition "User's income" may take one of three possible values: "lower than 1000", "between 1000 and 2000" and "more than 2000".

Simple actions take Boolean values "True" and "False" (e.g., the action "Admitted discount = 20%" takes the values "True" denoted by "X" if the action should occur and 'False' denoted by "-" if not). Just like with conditions, actions may also take values from other domains. For example, an action "Admitted discount" may take one of five possible values: 0%, 10%, 20%, 35% and 50%.

Decision table testing starts with designing decision tables based on the specification. Rules containing infeasible combinations of condition values are excluded or marked as "infeasible". Next, the Test Analyst should review the decision tables with the other stakeholders. The Test Analyst should ensure the rules within the table are consistent (i.e., the rules do not overlap), complete (i.e., they contain a rule for each feasible combination of condition values), and correct (i.e., they model the intended behavior).

The basic principle in decision table testing is that the rules form the test conditions.

When designing a test case to cover a given rule, the Test Analyst should be aware that the inputs of the test case might be different parameters than in the conditions of the decision table. For example, the `TRUE` value of the condition "age $\geq$ 18?" may require the tester to calculate the age from the input parameters birth date and current date. Similarly, the expected results of the test case may be indirect consequences of the actions of the decision table.

After the decision table is ready, the rules need to be implemented as test cases by selecting test input values (and expected results) that fulfil the conditions and actions.

Collapsed decision tables
When trying to test every possible input combination according to the conditions, decision tables can become very large. A complete limited-entry decision table with n conditions has 2^n rules. A technique of systematically reducing the number of combinations is called collapsed decision table testing [Mosley93]. When this technique is used, a group of rules with the same set of actions can be reduced (collapsed) to one rule if, within this group, some conditions are not relevant for the action, and all the other conditions remain unchanged. In this resulting rule the values of the irrelevant conditions are denoted as "don't care", usually marked with a dash "-". For conditions with "don't care" values, the Test Analyst may specify arbitrary valid values for test implementation.

Another case for collapsing rules is when a condition value is not applicable in combination with some other condition values or when two or more conditions have conflicting values. For example, in a decision table for card payments, if the condition "card is valid" is false, the condition "PIN code is correct" is not applicable.

Collapsed decision tables may have far fewer rules than full decision tables, which results in a lower number of test cases and less effort. If a given rule has "don't care" entries, and only one test case covers this rule, only one of several possible values of the condition will be tested for that rule, so a defect involving other values may remain undetected. Hence, for high risk levels, in alignment with the Test Manager, the Test Analyst should define separate rules for each feasible combination of the single condition values rather than collapsing the decision table.

Applicability
Decision table testing is commonly applied to integration, system, and acceptance test levels. It may also be applicable to component testing when a component is responsible for a set of decision logic. This technique is particularly useful when the test object is specified in the form of flowcharts or tables of business rules.

Decision tables are also a requirements definition technique and sometimes requirements specifications may already be defined in this format. The Test Analyst should still participate in reviewing the decision tables and analyze them before starting test design.

Limitations/Difficulties
When considering combinations of conditions, finding all the interacting conditions can be challenging, particularly when requirements are not well-defined or not documented at all. Care must be taken when selecting the conditions considered in a decision table so that the number of combinations of those conditions remains manageable. In the worst case, the number of rules will grow exponentially.

Coverage
The common coverage standard for this technique is to cover each rule of the decision table with one test case. The coverage is measured as the number of rules covered by the test suite divided by the total number of feasible rules, expressed as a percentage.

Boundary value analysis and equivalence partitioning can be combined with the decision table technique, especially in the case of extended-entry decision tables. If conditions contain equivalence partitions that are ordered, the boundary values may be used as additional entries leading to additional rules and test cases.

Types of Defects
Typical defects include incorrect logic-related processing based on particular combinations of conditions resulting in unexpected results. During the creation of the decision tables, defects may be found in the specification document. It is not unusual to prepare a set of conditions and determine that the expected result is unspecified for one or more rules. The most common types of defects are omissions of actions (i.e., there is no information regarding what should actually happen in a certain situation) and contradictions.

3.2.4 State Transition Testing

State transition testing is used to test the ability of the test object to enter and exit from defined states via valid transitions, as well as to try entering invalid states or covering invalid transitions. Events cause the test object to transition from state to state and to perform actions. Events may be qualified by conditions (sometimes called guard conditions or transition guards) which influence the transition path to be taken. For example, a login event with a valid username/password combination will result in a different transition than a login event with an invalid password. This information is represented in a state transition diagram or in a state transition table (which may also include potential invalid transitions between states).

Applicability
State transition testing is applicable for any software that has defined states and has events that will cause the transitions between those states (e.g., changing screens). State transition testing can be used at any test level. Embedded software, web software, and any type of transactional software are good candidates for this type of testing. Control systems, e.g., traffic light controllers, are also good candidates for this type of testing.

Limitations/Difficulties
Determining the states is often the most difficult part of defining the state transition diagram or state transition table. When the test object has a user interface, the various screens that are displayed for the user are often represented by states. For embedded software, the states may be dependent upon the states of the hardware.

Besides the states themselves, the basic unit of state transition testing is the individual transition. Simply testing all single transitions will find some kinds of state transition defects, but more may be found by testing sequences of transitions. A single transition is called a 0-switch; a sequence of two successive transitions is called a 1-switch; a sequence of three successive transitions is called a 2-switch, and so forth. In general, an N-switch represents N+1 successive transitions [Chow1978]. With N increasing, the number of N-switches grows very quickly, making it difficult to achieve N-switch coverage with a reasonable, small number of tests.

Coverage
As with other types of test techniques, there is a hierarchy of levels of coverage. The minimum acceptable degree of coverage is to have visited every state and traversed every transition at least once. 100% transition coverage (also known as 100% 0-switch coverage) will guarantee that every state is visited and every transition is traversed, unless the system design or the state transition model (diagram or table) is defective. Depending on the relationships between states and transitions, it may be necessary to traverse some transitions more than once in order to execute other transitions a single time.

The term "N-switch coverage" relates to the number of switches covered of length N+1, as a percentage of the total number of switches of that length. For example, achieving 100% 1-switch coverage requires that every valid sequence of two successive transitions has been tested at least once. This testing may trigger some types of failures that 100% 0-switch coverage would miss.

"Round-trip coverage" applies to situations in which sequences of transitions form loops. 100% round-trip coverage is achieved when all loops from any state back to the same state have been tested for all states at which loops begin and end. This loop cannot contain more than one occurrence of any particular state (except the initial/final one) [Offutt16].

For any of these approaches, an even higher degree of coverage will attempt to include all invalid transitions identified in a state transition table. Coverage requirements for state transition testing must identify whether invalid transitions are included.

Designing test cases to achieve the desired coverage is supported by the state transition diagram or the state transition table for the particular test object. This information may also be represented in a table that shows the N-switch transitions for a particular value of N [Black09].

A manual procedure may be applied for identifying the items to be covered (e.g., transitions, states or N-switches). One suggested method is to print the state transition diagram and state transition table and use a pen or pencil to mark up the items covered until the required coverage is shown [Black09]. This approach would become too time-consuming for more complex state transition diagrams and state transition tables. A tool should therefore be used to support state transition testing.

Types of Defects
Typical defects include the following (see also [Beizer95]):
- Incorrect event types or values
- Incorrect action types or values
- Incorrect initial state
- Inability to reach some exit state(s)
- Inability to enter required states
- Extra (unnecessary) states
- Inability to execute some valid transition(s) correctly
- Ability to execute invalid transitions
- Wrong guard conditions

During the creation of the state transition model, defects may be found in the specification document. The most common types of defects are omissions (i.e., there is no information regarding what should actually happen in a certain situation) and contradictions.

3.2.5 Classification Tree Technique

Classification trees support certain black-box test techniques by enabling a graphical representation of the data space to be created which applies to the test object.

The data is organized into classifications and classes as follows:
- Classifications: These represent parameters within the data space for the test object, such as input parameters (which can further contain environment states and pre-conditions), and output parameters. For example, if an application can be configured many different ways, the classifications might include client, browser, language, and operating system.
- Classes: Each classification can have any number of classes and sub-classes describing the occurrence of the parameter. Each class, or equivalence partition, is a specific value within a classification. In the above example, the language classification might include equivalence partitions for English, French and Spanish.

Classification trees allow the Test Analysts to enter combinations as they see fit. This includes, for example, pairwise combinations (see Section 3.2.6), three-wise combinations, and single-wise.

Additional information regarding the use of the classification tree technique is provided in [Bath14] and [Black09].

Applicability
The creation of a classification tree helps a Test Analyst to identify parameters (classifications) and their equivalence partitions (classes) which are of interest.

Further analysis of the classification tree diagram enables possible boundary values to be identified and certain combinations of inputs to be identified which are either of particular interest or may be discounted (e.g., because they are incompatible). The resulting classification tree may then be used to support equivalence partitioning, boundary value analysis or pairwise testing (see Section 3.2.6).

Limitations/Difficulties
As the quantity of classifications and/or classes increases, the diagram becomes larger and less easy to use. Also, the Classification Tree Technique does not create complete test cases, only test data

combinations. Test Analysts must supply the results for each test combination to create complete test cases.

Coverage
Test cases may be designed to achieve, for example, minimum class coverage (i.e., all values in a classification tested at least once). The Test Analyst may also decide to cover pairwise combinations or use other types of combinatorial testing, e.g. three-wise.

Types of Defects
The types of defects found depend on the technique(s) which the classification trees support (i.e., equivalence partitioning, boundary value analysis or pairwise testing).

3.2.6 Pairwise Testing

Pairwise testing is used when testing software in which several input parameters, each with several possible values, must be tested in combination, giving rise to more combinations than are feasible to test in the time allowed. The input parameters may be independent in the sense that any option for any factor (i.e., any selected value for any one input parameter) can be combined with any option for any other factor, however it is not always the case (see a note on feature models below). The combination of a specific parameter (variable or factor) with a specific value of that parameter is called a parameter- value pair (e.g., if 'color' is a parameter with seven permitted values including 'red', then 'color = red' could be a parameter-value pair).

Pairwise testing uses combinatorial techniques to ensure that each parameter-value pair gets tested once against each parameter-value pair of each other parameter (i.e., 'all pairs' of parameter-value pairs for any two different parameters get tested), while avoiding testing all combinations of parameter-value pairs. If the Test Analyst uses a manual approach, a table is constructed with test cases represented by rows and one column for each parameter. The Test Analyst then populates the table with values such that all pairs of values can be identified in the table (see [Black09]). Any entries in the table which are left blank can be filled with values by the Test Analyst using their own domain knowledge.

There are a number of tools available to aid a Test Analyst in this task (see www.pairwise.org for samples). They require, as input, a list of the parameters and their values and generate a suitable set of combinations of values from each parameter that covers all pairs of parameter-value pairs. The output of the tool can be used as input for test cases. Note that the Test Analyst must supply the expected results for each combination that is created by the tools.

Classification trees (see Section 3.2.5) are often used in conjunction with pairwise testing [Bath14] Classification tree design is supported by tools and enables combinations of parameters and their values to be visualized (some tools offer a pairwise enhancement). This helps to identify the following information:
- Inputs to be used by the pairwise test technique.
- Particular combinations of interest (e.g., frequently used or a common source of defects)
- Particular combinations which are incompatible. This does not assume that the combined factors won't affect each other; they very well might, but should affect each other in acceptable ways.
- Logical relationships between variables. For example, "if variable1 = x, then variable2 cannot be y". Classification trees which capture these relationships are called "feature models".

Applicability
The problem of having too many combinations of parameter values manifests itself in at least two different situations related to testing. Some test items involve several parameters each with a number of possible values, for instance a screen with several input fields. In this case, combinations of parameter

values make up the input data for the test cases. Furthermore, some systems may be configurable in a number of dimensions, resulting in a potentially large configuration space. In both these situations, pairwise testing can be used to identify a subset of combinations that is manageable and feasible.

For parameters with many values, equivalence partitioning, or some other selection mechanism may first be applied to each parameter individually to reduce the number of values for each parameter, before pairwise testing is applied to reduce the set of resulting combinations. Capturing the parameters and their values in a classification tree supports this activity.

These techniques are usually applied to the component integration, system and system integration test levels.

Limitations/Difficulties
The major limitation with these techniques is the assumption that the results of a few tests are representative of all tests and that those few tests represent expected usage. If there is an unexpected interaction between certain variables, it may go undetected with this test technique if that particular combination is not tested. These techniques can be difficult to explain to a non-technical audience as they may not understand the logical reduction of tests. Any such explanation should be balanced by mentioning the results from empirical studies [Kuhn16], which showed that in the area of medical devices under study, 66% of failures were triggered by a single variable and 97% by either one variable or two variables interacting. There is a residual risk that pairwise testing may not detect systems failures where three or more variables interact.

Identifying the parameters and their respective values is sometimes difficult to achieve. Therefore, this task should be performed with the support of classification trees where possible (see Section 3.2.5). Finding a minimal set of combinations to satisfy a certain level of coverage is difficult to do manually. Tools may be used to find the smallest possible set of combinations. Some tools support the ability to force some combinations to be included in or excluded from the final selection of combinations. A Test Analyst may use this capability to emphasize or de-emphasize factors based on domain knowledge or product usage information.

Coverage
The 100% pairwise coverage requires every pair of values of any pair of parameters be included in at least one combination.

Types of Defects
The most common type of defects found with this test technique is defects related to the combined values of two parameters.

3.2.7 Use Case Testing

Use case testing provides transactional, behavior-based tests that should emulate intended use of the component or system specified by the use case. Use cases are defined in terms of interactions between the actors and a component or system that accomplishes some goal. Actors can be human users, external hardware, or other components or systems.

A common standard for use cases is provided in [OMG-UML].

Applicability
Use case testing is usually applied in system and acceptance testing. It may also be used in integration testing if the behavior of the components or systems is specified by use cases. Use cases are also often the basis for performance testing because they portray realistic usage of the system. The behaviors

described in the use cases may be assigned to virtual users to create a realistic load on the system (so long as load and performance requirements are specified in them or for them).

Limitations/Difficulties
In order to be valid, the use cases must convey realistic user transactions. Use case specifications are a form of system design. The requirements of what users need to accomplish should come from users or user representatives, and should be checked against organizational requirements before designing corresponding use cases. The value of a use case is reduced if it does not reflect real user and organizational requirements, or hinders rather than assists completion of user tasks.

An accurate definition of the exception, alternative and error handling behaviors is important for the coverage to be thorough. Use cases should be taken as a guideline, but not a complete definition of what should be tested as they may not provide a clear definition of the entire set of requirements. It may also be beneficial to create other models, such as flowcharts and/or decision tables, from the use case narrative to improve the accuracy of the testing and to verify the use case itself. As with other forms of specification this is likely to reveal logical anomalies in the use case specification, if they exist.

Coverage
The minimum acceptable level of coverage of a use case is to have one test case for the basic behavior and sufficient additional test cases to cover each alternative and error handling behavior. If a minimal test suite is required, multiple alternative behaviors may be incorporated into a test case provided they are mutually compatible. If better diagnostic capability is required (e.g., to assist in isolating defects), one additional test case per alternative behavior may be designed, although nested alternative behaviors will still require some of those behaviors to be amalgamated into a single test case (e.g., termination versus non-termination alternative behaviors within a "retry" exception behavior).

Types of Defects
Defects include mishandling of defined behaviors, missed alternative behaviors, incorrect processing of the conditions presented and poorly implemented or incorrect error messages.

3.2.8 Combining Techniques

Sometimes techniques are combined to create test cases. For example, the conditions identified in a decision table might be subjected to equivalence partitioning to discover multiple ways in which a condition might be satisfied. Test cases would then cover not only every combination of conditions, but also, for those conditions which are partitioned, additional test cases should be generated to cover the equivalence partitions. When selecting the particular technique to be applied, the Test Analyst should consider the applicability of the technique, the limitations and difficulties, and the goals of the testing in terms of coverage and defects to be detected. These aspects are described for the individual techniques covered in this chapter. There may not be a single "best" technique for a situation. Combining the suitable techniques will often be the most effective way to achieve the test objectives set, assuming there is sufficient time and skill to correctly apply the techniques.

3.3 Experience-Based Test Techniques

Experience-based testing utilizes the skill and intuition of the testers, along with their experience with similar applications or technologies to target testing in order to increase defect detection. These test techniques range from "quick tests" in which the tester has no formally pre-planned activities to perform, through pre-planned test sessions using test charters to scripted testing sessions. They are almost always useful, but have particular value when aspects included in the following list of advantages can be achieved.

Experience-based testing has the following advantages:

- It may be a good alternative to more structured approaches in cases where system documentation is lacking.
- It can be applied when testing time is severely restricted.
- It enables available expertise in the domain and technology to be applied in testing. This may include those not involved in testing, e.g., from business analysts, customers or clients.
- It can provide early feedback to the developers.
- It helps the team become familiar with the software as it is produced.
- It is effective when operational failures are analyzed.
- It enables a diversity of test techniques to be applied.

Experience-based testing has the following disadvantages:
- It may be inappropriate in systems requiring detailed test documentation.
- High levels of repeatability are difficult to achieve.
- The ability to precisely assess coverage is limited.
- Tests are less suited for subsequent automation.

When using reactive and heuristic approaches, testers normally use experience-based testing, which is more reactive to events than pre-planned test approaches. In addition, execution and evaluation are concurrent tasks. Some structured approaches to experience-based testing are not entirely dynamic, i.e., the tests are not created entirely at the same time as the tester executes the test. This might be the case, for example, where error guessing is used to target particular aspects of the test object before test execution.

Note that although some ideas on coverage are presented for the techniques discussed here, experience-based test techniques do not have formal coverage criteria.

3.3.1 Error Guessing

When using the error guessing technique, a Test Analyst uses experience to guess the potential errors that might have been made when the code was being designed and developed. When the expected errors have been identified, a Test Analyst then determines the best methods to use to uncover the resulting defects. For example, if a Test Analyst expects the software will exhibit failures when an invalid password is entered, tests will be run to enter a variety of different values in the password field to verify if the error was indeed made and has resulted in a defect that can be seen as a failure when the tests are run.

In addition to being used as a test technique, error guessing is also useful during risk analysis to identify potential failure modes. [Myers11]

Applicability
Error guessing is done primarily during integration and system testing, but can be used at any test level. This technique is often used with other techniques and helps to broaden the scope of the existing test cases. Error guessing can also be used effectively when testing a new release of the software to test for common defects before starting more rigorous and scripted testing.

Limitations/Difficulties
The following limitations and difficulties apply to error guessing:
- Coverage is difficult to assess and varies widely with the capability and experience of the Test Analyst.
- It is best used by an experienced tester who is familiar with the types of defects that are commonly introduced in the type of code being tested.

- It is commonly used, but is frequently not documented and so may be less reproducible than other forms of testing.
- Test cases may be documented but in a way that only the author understands and can reproduce.

Coverage

When a defect taxonomy is used, coverage is determined by taking the number of taxonomy items tested divided by the total number of taxonomy items and stating coverage as a percentage. Without a defect taxonomy, coverage is limited by the experience and knowledge of the tester and the time available. The quantity of defects found from this technique will vary based on how well the tester can target problematic areas.

Types of Defects

Typical defects are usually those defined in the particular defect taxonomy or "guessed" by the Test Analyst, that might not have been found in black-box testing.

3.3.2 Checklist-Based Testing

When applying the checklist-based test technique, an experienced Test Analyst uses a high-level, generalized list of items to be noted, checked, or remembered, or a set of rules or criteria against which a test object has to be verified. These checklists are built based on a set of standards, experience, and other considerations. For example, a user interface standard checklist can be employed as the basis for testing an application. In Agile software development, checklists can be built from the acceptance criteria for a user story.

Applicability

Checklist-based testing is most effective in projects with an experienced test team that is familiar with the software under test or familiar with the area covered by the checklist (e.g., to successfully apply a user interface checklist, the Test Analyst may be familiar with user interface testing but not the specific system under test). Because checklists are high-level and tend to lack the detailed steps commonly found in test cases and test procedures, the knowledge of the tester is used to fill in the gaps. By removing the detailed steps, checklists are low maintenance and can be applied to multiple similar releases.

Checklists are well-suited to projects where software is released and changed quickly. This helps to reduce both the preparation and maintenance time for test documentation. They can be used for any test level and are also used for regression testing and smoke testing.

Limitations/Difficulties

The high-level nature of the checklists can affect the reproducibility of test results. It is possible that several testers will interpret the checklists differently and will follow different approaches to fulfil the checklist items. This may cause different test results, even though the same checklist is used. This can result in wider coverage but reproducibility is sometimes sacrificed. Checklists may also result in over- confidence regarding the level of coverage that is achieved since the actual testing depends on the tester's judgment. Checklists can be derived from more detailed test cases or lists and tend to grow over time. Maintenance is required to ensure that the checklists are covering the important aspects of the software under test.

Coverage

Coverage can be determined by taking the number of checklist items tested divided by the total number of checklist items and stating coverage as a percentage. The coverage is as good as the checklist but, because of the high-level nature of the checklist, the results will vary based on the Test Analyst who executes the checklist.

Types of Defects
Typical defects found with this technique cause failures resulting from varying the data, the sequence of steps or the general workflow during testing.

3.3.3 Exploratory Testing

Exploratory testing is characterized by the tester simultaneously learning about the test object and its defects, planning the testing work to be done, designing and executing the tests, and reporting the results. The tester dynamically adjusts test goals during execution and prepares only lightweight documentation. [Whittaker09]

Applicability
Good exploratory testing is planned, interactive, and creative. It requires little documentation about the system to be tested and is often used in situations where the documentation is not available or is not adequate for other test techniques. Exploratory testing is often used to add to other test techniques and to serve as a basis for the development of additional test cases. Exploratory testing is frequently used in Agile software development to get user story testing done flexibly and quickly with only minimal documentation. However, the technique may also be applied to projects using a sequential development model.

Limitations/Difficulties
Exploratory testing does not provide any coverage measure. Moreover, reproducing the tests performed can be difficult. Using test charters to designate the areas to be covered in a test session and time- boxing to determine the time allowed for the testing are techniques used to manage exploratory testing. At the end of a test session or set of test sessions, the Test Manager may hold a debriefing session to gather the test results and determine the test charters for the next test sessions.

Another difficulty with exploratory testing sessions is to accurately track them in a test management system. This is sometimes done by creating test cases that are actually exploratory testing sessions. This allows the time allocated for the exploratory testing and the planned coverage to be tracked with the other test efforts.

Since reproducibility may be difficult to achieve with exploratory testing, this can also cause problems when needing to recall the steps to reproduce a failure. Some organizations use the capture/playback capability of a test automation tool to record the steps taken by an exploratory tester. This provides a complete record of all activities during the exploratory testing session (or any experience-based testing session). Analyzing the details to find the actual cause of a failure can be tedious, but at least there is a record of all the steps that were involved.

Others tools may be used to capture exploratory testing sessions but these don't record the expected results because they don't capture the GUI interaction. In this case the expected results must be noted down so that proper analysis of defects can be undertaken if needed. In general, it is recommended that notes also be taken while performing exploratory testing, to support reproducibility where required.

Coverage
Test charters may be designed for specific tasks, objectives, and deliverables. Exploratory testing sessions are then planned to achieve those criteria. The charter may also identify where to focus the test effort, what is in and out of scope of the test session, and what resources should be committed to complete the planned tests. A test session may be used to focus on particular defect types and other potentially problematic areas that can be addressed without the formality of scripted testing.

Types of Defects
Typical defects found with exploratory testing are scenario-based issues that are missed during scripted functional suitability testing, issues that fall between functional boundaries, and workflow related issues. Performance and security issues are also sometimes uncovered during exploratory testing.

3.3.4 Defect-Based Test Techniques

A defect-based test technique is one in which the type of defect sought is used as the basis for test design, with tests derived systematically from what is known about the type of defect. Unlike black-box testing which derives its tests from the test basis, defect-based testing derives tests from lists which focus on defects. In general, the lists may be organized into defect types, root causes, failure symptoms and other defect-related data. Standard lists apply to multiple types of software and are not product specific. Using these lists helps to leverage industry standard knowledge to derive the particular tests. By adhering to industry-specific lists, metrics regarding defect occurrence can be tracked across projects and even across organizations. The most common defect lists are those which are organization or project specific and make use of specific expertise and experience.

Defect-based testing may also use lists of identified risks and risk scenarios as a basis for targeting testing. This test technique allows a Test Analyst to target a specific type of defect or to work systematically through a list of known and common defects of a particular type. From this information, the Test Analyst creates the test conditions and test cases that will cause the defect to manifest itself (if it exists).

Applicability
Defect-based testing can be applied at any test level but is most commonly applied during system testing.

Limitations/Difficulties
Multiple defect taxonomies exist and may be focused on particular types of testing, such as usability. It is important to pick a taxonomy that is applicable to the software under test (if any are available). For example, there may not be any taxonomies available for innovative software. Some organizations have compiled their own taxonomies of likely or frequently seen defects. Whatever defect taxonomy is used, it is important to define the expected coverage prior to starting the testing.

Coverage
The technique provides coverage criteria which are used to determine when all the useful test cases have been identified. Coverage items may be structural elements, specification elements, usage scenarios, or any combination of these, depending on the defect list. As a practical matter, the coverage criteria for defect-based test techniques tend to be less systematic than for black-box test techniques in that only general rules for coverage are given and the specific decision about what constitutes the limit of useful coverage is discretionary. As with other techniques, the coverage criteria do not mean that the entire set of tests is complete, but rather that defects being considered no longer suggest any useful tests based on that technique.

Types of Defects
The types of defects discovered usually depend on the defect taxonomy in use. For example, if a user interface defect list is used, the majority of the discovered defects would likely be user interface related, but other defects can be discovered as a by-product of the specific testing.

3.4 Applying the Most Appropriate Technique

Black-box and experience-based test techniques are most effective when used together. Experience-based test techniques fill the gaps in achieving test objectives that result from any systematic weaknesses in black-box test techniques.

There is not one perfect technique for all situations. It is important for the Test Analyst to understand the advantages and disadvantages of each technique and to be able to select the best technique or set of techniques for the situation, considering the project type, schedule, access to information, skills of the tester and other factors that can influence the selection.

In the discussion of each black-box and experience-based test technique (see Sections 3.2 and 3.3 respectively), the information provided in "applicability", "limitations/difficulties" and "coverage" guides a Test Analyst in selecting the most appropriate test techniques to apply.

4. Testing Software Quality Characteristics - 180 mins.

Keywords
accessibility, compatibility, functional appropriateness, functional completeness, functional correctness, functional suitability, interoperability, learnability, operability, Software Usability Measurement Inventory (SUMI), usability, user error protection, user experience, user interface aesthetics, Website Analysis and MeasureMent Inventory (WAMMI)

Learning Objectives for Testing Software Quality Characteristics

4.1 Introduction
No learning objectives

4.2 Quality Characteristics for Business Domain Testing

TA-4.2.1 (K2) Explain what test techniques are appropriate to test the functional completeness, functional correctness and functional appropriateness

TA-4.2.2 (K2) Define the typical defects to be targeted for the functional completeness, functional correctness and functional appropriateness characteristics

TA-4.2.3 (K2) Define when the functional completeness, correctness and appropriateness characteristics should be tested in the software development lifecycle

TA-4.2.4 (K2) Explain the approaches that would be suitable to verify and validate both the implementation of the usability requirements and the fulfillment of the user's expectations

TA-4.2.5 (K2) Explain the role of the Test Analyst in interoperability testing including identification of the defects to be targeted

TA-4.2.6 (K2) Explain the role of the Test Analyst in portability testing including identification of the defects to be targeted

TA-4.2.7 (K4) For a given set of requirements, determine the test conditions required to verify the functional and/or non-functional quality characteristics within the scope of the Test Analyst

4.1 Introduction

While the previous chapter described specific techniques available to the tester, this chapter considers the application of those techniques in evaluating the characteristics used to describe the quality of software applications or systems.

This syllabus discusses the quality characteristics which may be evaluated by a Test Analyst. The attributes to be evaluated by the Technical Test Analyst are considered in the Advanced Technical Test Analyst syllabus [CTAL-TTA].

The description of product quality characteristics provided in ISO 25010 [ISO25010] is used as a guide to describe the characteristics. The ISO software quality model divides product quality into different product quality characteristics, each of which may have sub-characteristics. These are shown in the table below, together with an indication of which characteristics/sub-characteristics are covered by the Test Analyst and Technical Test Analyst syllabi:

Characteristic	Sub-Characteristics	Test Analyst	Technical Test Analyst
Functional suitability	Functional correctness, functional appropriateness, functional completeness	X	
Reliability	Maturity, fault-tolerance, recoverability, availability		X
Usability	Appropriateness recognizability, learnability, operability, user interface aesthetics, user error protection, accessibility	X	
Performance efficiency	Time behavior, resource utilization, capacity		X
Maintainability	Analyzability, modifiability, testability, modularity, reusability		X
Portability	Adaptability, installability, replaceability	X	X
Security	Confidentiality, integrity, non-repudiation, accountability, authenticity		X
Compatibility	Co-existence		X
	Interoperability	X	

While this allocation of work may vary in different organizations, it is the one that is followed in the associated ISTQB® syllabi.

For all of the quality characteristics and sub-characteristics discussed in this section, the typical risks must be recognized so that an appropriate test strategy can be formed and documented. Quality characteristic testing requires particular attention to SDLC timing, required tools, software and documentation availability, and technical expertise. Without a strategy to deal with each characteristic and its unique testing needs, the tester may not have adequate planning, ramp up and test execution time built into the schedule [Bath14]. Some of this testing, e.g., usability testing, can require allocation of special human resources, extensive planning, dedicated labs, specific tools, specialized testing skills and, in most cases, a significant amount of time. In some cases, usability testing may be performed by a separate group of usability or user experience experts.

While the Test Analyst may not be responsible for the quality characteristics that require a more technical approach, it is important that the Test Analyst is aware of the other characteristics and understands the overlapping areas for testing. For example, a test object that fails performance testing may likely fail in usability testing if it is too slow for the user to use effectively. Similarly, a test object with interoperability issues with some components is probably not ready for portability testing as that will tend to obscure the more basic problems when the environment is changed.

4.2 Quality Characteristics for Business Domain Testing

Functional suitability testing is a primary focus for the Test Analyst. Functional suitability testing is focused on "what" the test object does. The test basis for functional suitability testing is generally requirements, a specification, specific domain expertise or implied need. Functional suitability tests vary according to the test level in which they are conducted and can also be influenced by the SDLC. For example, a functional suitability test conducted during integration testing will test the functional suitability of interfacing components which implement a single defined function. At the system test level, functional suitability tests include testing the functional suitability of the system as a whole. For systems of systems, functional suitability testing will focus primarily on end-to-end testing across the integrated systems. A wide variety of test techniques are employed during functional suitability testing (see Chapter 3).

In Agile software development, functional suitability testing usually includes the following:
- Testing the specific functionality (e.g., user stories) planned for implementation in the particular iteration
- Regression testing for all unchanged functionality

In addition to the functional suitability testing covered in this section, there are also certain quality characteristics that are part of the Test Analyst's area of responsibility that are considered to be non-functional (focused on "how" the test object delivers the functionality) testing areas.

4.2.1 Functional Correctness Testing

Functional correctness involves verifying the application's adherence to the specified or implied requirements and may also include computational accuracy. Functional correctness testing employs many of the test techniques explained in Chapter 3 and often uses the specification or a legacy system as the test oracle. Functional correctness testing can be conducted at any test level and is targeted on incorrect handling of data or situations.

4.2.2 Functional Appropriateness Testing

Functional appropriateness testing involves evaluating and validating the appropriateness of a set of functions for its intended specified tasks. This testing can be based on the functional design (e.g., use cases and/or user stories). Functional appropriateness testing is usually conducted during system testing, but may also be conducted during the later stages of integration testing. Defects discovered in this testing are indications that the system will not be able to meet the needs of the user in a way that will be considered acceptable.

4.2.3 Functional Completeness Testing

Functional completeness testing is performed to determine the coverage of specified tasks and user objectives by the implemented functionality. Traceability between specification items (e.g., requirements, user stories, use cases) and the implemented functionality (e.g., function, component, workflow) is essential to enable required functional completeness to be determined. Measuring functional completeness may vary according to the particular test level and/or the SDLC used. For example, functional completeness for Agile software development may be based on implemented user stories and features. Functional completeness for system integration testing may focus on the coverage of high-level business processes.

Determining functional completeness is generally supported by test management tools if the Test Analyst is maintaining the traceability between the test cases and the functional specification items. Lower than expected levels of functional completeness are indications that the system has not been fully implemented.

4.2.4 Interoperability Testing

Interoperability testing verifies the exchange of information between two or more systems or components. Tests focus on the ability to exchange information and subsequently use the information that has been exchanged. Testing should cover all the intended target environments (including variations in the hardware, software, middleware, operating system, etc.) to ensure the data exchange will work properly. In reality, this may only be feasible for a relatively small number of environments. In that case interoperability testing may be limited to a selected representative group of environments. Specifying tests for interoperability requires that combinations of the intended target environments are identified, configured and available to the test team. These environments are then tested using a selection of functional suitability test cases which exercise the various data exchange points present in the environment.

Interoperability relates to how different components and software systems interact with each other. Software with good interoperability characteristics can be integrated with a number of other systems without requiring major changes or significant impact on non-functional behaviour. The number of changes and the effort required to implement and test those changes may be used as a measure of interoperability.

Testing for software interoperability may, for example, focus on the following design features:
- Use of industry-wide communications standards, such as XML
- Ability to automatically detect the communication needs of the systems it interacts with and adjust accordingly

Interoperability testing may be particularly significant for the following:
- Commercial off-the-shelf software products and tools
- Applications based on a system of systems
- Systems based on the Internet of Things
- Web services with connectivity to other systems

This type of testing is performed during component integration and system integration testing. At the system integration level, this type of testing is conducted to determine how well the fully developed system interacts with other systems. Because systems may interoperate on multiple levels, the Test Analyst must understand these interactions and be able to create the conditions that will exercise the various interactions. For example, if two systems will exchange data, the Test Analyst must be able to create the necessary data and the transactions required to perform the data exchange. It is important to remember that all interactions may not be clearly specified in the requirements documents. Instead, many of these interactions will be defined only in the system architecture and design documents. The Test Analyst must be able and prepared to examine these documents to determine the points of information exchange between systems and between the system and its environment to ensure all are tested. Techniques such as equivalence partitioning, boundary value analysis, decision tables, state transition diagrams, use cases and pairwise testing are all applicable to interoperability testing. Typical defects found include incorrect data exchange between interacting components.

4.2.5 Usability Evaluation

Test Analysts are often in the position to coordinate and support the evaluation of usability. This may include specifying usability tests or acting as a moderator working with the users to conduct tests. To do this effectively, a Test Analyst must understand the principal aspects, goals and approaches involved in these types of testing. Please refer to the ISTQB® Specialist syllabus in usability testing [ISTQB_UT_SYL] for details beyond the description provided in this section.

It is important to understand why users might have difficulty using the system or do not have a positive user experience (UX) (e.g., with using software for entertainment). To gain this understanding it is first necessary to appreciate that the term "user" may apply to a wide range of different types of personas, ranging from IT experts to children to people with disabilities.

4.2.5.1 Usability Aspects
The following are the three aspects considered in this section:
- Usability in the sense according to the ISO 25010 standard
- User experience (UX) as a generalization of usability
- Accessibility as a sub-characteristic of usability

Usability
Usability testing targets software defects that impact a user's ability to perform tasks via the user interface. Such defects may affect the user's ability to achieve their goals effectively, or efficiently, or with satisfaction. Usability problems can lead to confusion, error, delay or outright failure to complete some task on the part of the user.

The following are the sub-characteristics of usability [ISO 25010]; for their definitions, see [ISTQB_GLOSSARY]:
- Appropriateness recognizability (i.e., understandability)
- Learnability
- Operability
- User interface aesthetics (i.e., attractiveness)
- User error protection
- Accessibility (see below)

User Experience (UX)
User experience evaluation addresses the whole user experience with the test object, not just the direct interaction. This is of particular importance for test objects where factors such as enjoyment and user satisfaction are critical for business success.

Typical factors which influence user experience include the following:
- Brand image (i.e., the user's trust in the manufacturer)
- Interactive behavior
- The helpfulness of the test object, including help system, support and training

Accessibility
It is important to consider the accessibility to software for those with particular needs or restrictions for its use. This includes those with disabilities. Accessibility testing should consider the relevant standards, such as the Web Content Accessibility Guidelines (WCAG), and legislation, such as the Disability Discrimination Acts (Northern Ireland, Australia), Equality Act 2010 (England, Scotland, Wales) and Section 508 (US). Accessibility, similar to usability, must be considered when conducting design activities. Testing often occurs during the integration levels and continues through system testing and into the acceptance testing levels. Defects are usually determined when the software fails to meet the designated regulations or standards defined for the software.

Typical measures to improve accessibility focus on the opportunities provided for users with disabilities to interact with the application. These include the following:
- Voice recognition for inputs
- Ensuring that non-text content that is presented to the user has an equivalent text alternative

- Enabling text to be resized without loss of content or functionality

Accessibility guidelines support the Test Analyst by providing a source of information and checklists which can be used for testing (examples of accessibility guidelines are given in [ISTQB_UT_SYL]). In addition, tools and browser plugins are available to help testers identify accessibility issues, such as poor color choice in web pages that violate guidelines for color blindness.

4.2.5.2 Usability Evaluation Approaches
Usability, user experience and accessibility may be tested by one or more of the following approaches:
- Usability testing
- Usability reviews
- User surveys and questionnaires

Usability Testing
Usability testing evaluates the ease by which users can use or learn to use the system to reach a specified goal in a specific context. Usability testing is directed at measuring the following:
- Effectiveness - capability of the test object to enable users to achieve specified goals with accuracy and completeness in a specified context of use
- Efficiency - capability of the test object to enable users to expend appropriate amounts of resources in relation to the effectiveness achieved in a specified context of use
- Satisfaction - capability of the test object to satisfy users in a specified context of use

It is important to note that designing and specifying usability tests is often conducted by the Test Analyst in co-operation with testers who have special usability testing skills, and usability design engineers who understand the human-centered design process (see [ISTQB_UT_SYL] for details).

Usability Reviews
Inspections and reviews are a type of testing conducted from a usability perspective which help to increase the user's level of involvement. This can be cost effective by finding usability problems in requirements specifications and designs early in the SDLC. Heuristic evaluation (systematic inspection of a user interface design for usability) can be used to find the usability problems in the design so that they can be addressed as part of an iterative design process. This involves having a small set of evaluators examine the interface and judge its compliance with recognized usability principles (the "heuristics"). Reviews are more effective when the user interface is more visible. For example, sample screen shots are usually easier to understand and interpret than just describing the functionality given by a particular screen. Visualization is important for an adequate usability review of the documentation.

User Surveys and Questionnaires
Survey and questionnaire techniques may be applied to gather observations and feedback regarding user behavior with the system. Standardized and publicly available surveys such as Software Usability Measurement Inventory (SUMI) and Website Analysis and MeasureMent Inventory (WAMMI) permit benchmarking against a database of previous usability measurements. In addition, since SUMI provides tangible measurements of usability, this can provide a set of completion / acceptance criteria.

4.2.6 Portability Testing

Portability tests relate to the degree to which a software component or system can be transferred into its intended environment, either as a new installation, or from an existing environment.

The ISO 25010 classification of product quality characteristics includes the following sub-characteristics of portability:
- Installability
- Adaptability

- Replaceability

The task of identifying risks and designing tests for portability characteristics is shared between the Test Analyst and the Technical Test Analyst (see [ISTQB_ALTTA_SYL] Section 4.7).

4.2.6.1 Installability Testing
Installability testing is conducted on the software and written procedures are used to install and de-install the software on its target environment.

The typical testing objectives that are the focus of the Test Analyst include:
- Validating that different configurations of the software can be successfully installed. Where a large number of parameters may be configured, the Test Analyst may design tests using the pairwise technique to reduce the number of parameter combinations tested and focus on particular configurations of interest (e.g., those frequently used).
- Testing the functional correctness of installation and de-installation procedures.
- Performing functional suitability tests following an installation or de-installation to detect any defects which may have been introduced (e.g., incorrect configurations, functions not available).
- Identifying usability issues in installation and de-installation procedures (e.g., to validate that users are provided with understandable instructions and feedback/error messages when executing the procedure).

4.2.6.2 Adaptability Testing
Adaptability testing checks whether a given application can be adapted effectively and efficiently to function correctly in all intended target environments (hardware, software, middleware, operating system, cloud, etc.). The Test Analyst supports adaptability testing by identifying the intended target environments (e.g., versions of different mobile operating systems supported, different versions of browsers which may be used), and designing tests that cover combinations of these environments. The target environments are then tested using a selection of functional suitability test cases which exercise the various components present in the environment.

4.2.6.3 Replaceability Testing
Replaceability testing focuses on the ability of software components or versions within a system to be exchanged for others. This may be particularly relevant for system architectures based on the Internet of Things, where the exchange of different hardware devices and/or software installations is a common occurrence. For example, a hardware device used in a warehouse to register and control stock levels may be replaced by a more advanced hardware device (e.g., with a better scanner) or the installed software may be upgraded with a new version that enables stock replacement orders to be automatically issued to a supplier's system.

Replaceability tests may be performed by the Test Analyst in parallel with functional integration tests where more than one alternative component is available for integration into the complete system.

5. Reviews - 120 mins.

Keywords
checklist-based reviewing

Learning Objectives for Reviews

5.1 Introduction
No learning objectives

5.2 Using Checklists in Reviews
TA-5.2.1 (K3) Identify problems in a requirements specification according to checklist information provided in the syllabus

TA-5.2.2 (K3) Identify problems in a user story according to checklist information provided in the syllabus

5.1 Introduction

Test Analysts must be active participants in the review process, providing their unique views. When done properly, reviews can be the single biggest, and most cost-effective, contributor to overall delivered quality.

5.2 Using Checklists in Reviews

Checklist-based reviewing is the most common technique used by a Test Analyst when reviewing the test basis. Checklists are used during reviews to remind the participants to check specific points during the review. They can also help to de-personalize the review (e.g., " This is the same checklist we use for every review. We are not targeting only your work product.").

Checklist-based reviewing can be performed generically for all reviews or can focus on specific quality characteristics, areas or types of documents. For example, a generic checklist might verify the general document properties such as having a unique identifier, no references marked "to be determined", proper formatting and similar conformance items. A specific checklist for a requirements document might contain checks for the proper use of the terms "shall" and "should", checks for the testability of each stated requirement, and so forth.

The format of the requirements may also indicate the type of checklist to be used. A requirements document that is in narrative text format will have different review criteria than one that is based on diagrams.

Checklists may also be oriented toward a particular aspect, such as:
- A programmer/architect skill set or a tester skill set - in the case of the Test Analyst, the tester skill set checklist would be the most appropriate
- A certain risk level (e.g., in safety-critical systems) - the checklists will typically include the specific information needed for the risk level
- A specific test technique - the checklist will focus on the information needed for a particular technique (e.g., rules to be represented in a decision table)
- A particular specification item, such as a requirement, use case or user story - these are discussed in the following sections and generally have a different focus than those used by a Technical Test Analyst for the review of code or architecture

5.2.1 Requirements Reviews

The following items are an example of what a requirements-oriented checklist could include:
- Source of the requirement (e.g., person, department)
- Testability of each requirement
- Priority of each requirement
- Acceptance criteria for each requirement
- Availability of a use case calling structure, if applicable
- Unique identification of each requirement/use case/user story
- Versioning of each requirement/use case/user story
- Traceability for each requirement from business/marketing requirements
- Traceability between requirements and/or use cases (if applicable)
- Use of consistent terminology (e.g., uses a glossary)

It is important to remember that if a requirement is not testable, meaning that it is defined in such a way that the Test Analyst cannot determine how to test it, then there is a defect in that requirement. For example, a requirement that states "The software should be very user friendly" is untestable. How can the Test Analyst determine if the software is user friendly, or even very user-friendly? If, instead, the requirement says "The software must conform to the usability standards stated in the usability standards document, version xxx", and if the usability standards document exists, then this is a testable requirement. It is also an overarching requirement because this one requirement applies to every item in the interface. In this case, this one requirement could easily spawn many individual test cases in a non-trivial application. Traceability from this requirement, or perhaps from the usability standards document, to the test cases, is also critical because if the referenced usability specification should change, all the test cases will need to be reviewed and updated as needed.

A requirement is also untestable if the tester is unable to determine whether the test passed or failed, or is unable to construct a test that can pass or fail. For example, "System shall be available 100% of the time, 24 hours per day, 7 days per week, 365 (or 366) days a year" is untestable.

A simple checklist[1] for use case reviews may include the following questions:
- Is the basic behavior (path) clearly defined?
- Are all alternative behaviors (paths) identified, complete with error handling?
- Are the user interface messages defined?
- Is there only one basic behavior (there should be, otherwise there are multiple use cases)?
- Is each behavior testable?

5.2.2 User Story Reviews

In Agile software development, requirements usually take the form of user stories. These stories represent small units of demonstrable functionality. Whereas a use case is a user transaction that traverses multiple areas of functionality, a user story is a more isolated feature and is generally scoped by the time it takes to develop it. A checklist[1] for a user story could include the following:
- Is the story appropriate for the target iteration/sprint?
- Is the story written from the view of the person who is requesting it?
- Are the acceptance criteria defined and testable?
- Is the feature clearly defined and distinct?
- Is the story independent of any others?
- Is the story prioritized?
- Does the story follow the commonly used format:
  As a < type of user >, I want < some goal > so that < some reason > [Cohn04]

If the story defines a new interface, then using a generic story checklist (such as the one above) and a detailed user interface checklist would be appropriate.

5.2.3 Tailoring Checklists

A checklist can be tailored based on the following:
- Organization (e.g., considering company policies, standards, conventions, legal constraints)
- Project/development effort (e.g., focus, technical standards, risks)
- The type of work product being reviewed (e.g., code reviews might be tailored to specific programming languages)
- The risk level of the work product being reviewed
- Test techniques to be used

Good checklists will find problems and will also help to start discussions regarding other items that might not have been specifically referenced in the checklist. Using a combination of checklists is a strong way

---

[1] The exam question will provide a subset of the use case checklist with which to answer the question

to ensure a review achieves the highest quality work product. Using checklist-based reviewing with standard checklists such as those referenced in the Foundation Level syllabus and developing organizationally specific checklists such as the ones shown above will help the Test Analyst be effective in reviews.

For more information on reviews and inspections see [Gilb93] and [Wiegers03]. Further examples of checklists can be obtained from the references in Section 7.4.

6. Test Tools and Automation - 90 mins.

Keywords
keyword-driven testing, test data preparation, test design, test execution, test script

Learning Objectives for Test Tools and Automation

6.1 Introduction
No learning objectives

6.2 Keyword-Driven Testing
TA-6.2.1 (K3) For a given scenario determine the appropriate activities for a Test Analyst in a keyword-driven testing project

6.3 Types of Test Tools
TA-6.3.1 (K2) Explain the usage and types of test tools applied in test design, test data preparation and test execution

6.1 Introduction

Test tools can greatly improve the efficiency and accuracy of testing. The test tools and automation approaches which are used by a Test Analyst are described in this chapter. It should be noted that Test Analysts work together with developers, Test Automation Engineers and Technical Test Analysts to create test automation solutions. Keyword-driven testing in particular involves the Test Analyst and leverages their experience with the business and the system functionality.

Further information on the subject of test automation and the role of the Test Automation Engineer is provided in the ISTQB® Advanced Level Test Automation Engineer syllabus [ISTQB_TAE_SYL].

6.2 Keyword-Driven Testing

Keyword-driven testing is one of the principal test automation approaches and involves the Test Analyst in providing the main inputs: keywords and data.

Keywords (sometimes referred to as action words) are mostly, but not exclusively, used to represent high-level business interactions with a system (e.g., "cancel order"). Each keyword is typically used to represent a number of detailed interactions between an actor and the system under test. Sequences of keywords (including relevant test data) are used to specify test cases [Buwalda02].

In test automation a keyword is implemented as one or more executable test scripts. Tools read test cases written as a sequence of keywords that call the appropriate test scripts which implement the keyword functionality. The scripts are implemented in a highly modular manner to enable easy mapping to specific keywords. Programming skills are needed to implement these modular scripts.

The following are the primary advantages of keyword-driven testing:
- Keywords that relate to a particular application or business domain can be defined by domain experts. This can make the task of test case specification more efficient.
- A person with primarily domain expertise can benefit from automatic test case execution (once the keywords have been implemented as scripts) without having to understand the underlying automation code.
- Using a modular writing technique enables efficient maintenance of test cases by the Test Automation Engineer when changes to the functionality and to the interface to the software under test occur [Bath14].
- Test case specifications are independent of their implementation.

Test Analysts usually create and maintain the keyword/action word data. They must realize that the task of script development is still necessary for implementing the keywords. Once the keywords and data to be used have been defined, the test automator (e.g., Technical Test Analyst or Test Automation Engineer) translates the business process keywords and lower-level actions into automated test scripts.

While keyword-driven testing is usually run during system testing, code development may start as early as the test design. In an iterative environment, particularly when continuous integration/continuous deployment are used, test automation development is a continuous process.

Once the input keywords and data are created, the Test Analyst assumes responsibility to execute the test scripts containing the keywords and to analyze any failures that may occur.

When an anomaly is detected, the Test Analyst should assist in investigating the cause of failure to determine if the defect is with the keywords, the input data, the test automation script itself or with the application being tested. Usually, the first step in troubleshooting is to execute the same test with the same data manually to see if the failure is in the application itself. If this does not show a failure, the Test Analyst should review the sequence of tests that led up to the failure to determine if the problem occurred in a previous step (perhaps by introducing incorrect input data), but the defect did not surface until later in the processing. If the Test Analyst is unable to determine the cause of failure, the trouble- shooting information should be passed to the Technical Test Analyst or developer for further analysis.

6.3 Types of Test Tools

Much of a Test Analyst's job requires the effective use of tools. This effectiveness is enhanced by the following:
- Knowing which tools to use
- Knowing that tools can increase the efficiency of the test effort (e.g., by helping to provide better coverage in the time allowed)

6.3.1 Test Design Tools

Test design tools are used to help create test cases and test data to be applied for testing. These tools may work from specific requirements document formats, models (e.g., UML), or inputs provided by the Test Analyst. Test design tools are often designed and built to work with particular formats and particular tools such as specific requirements management tools.

Test design tools can provide information for the Test Analyst to use when determining the types of tests that are needed to obtain the particular targeted level of coverage, confidence in the system, or product risk mitigation actions. For example, classification tree tools generate (and display) the set of combinations that is needed to reach full coverage based on a selected coverage criterion. This information then can be used by the Test Analyst to determine the test cases that must be executed.

6.3.2 Test Data Preparation Tools

Test data preparation tools can provide the following benefits:
- Analyze a document such as a requirements document or even the source code to determine the data required during testing to achieve a level of coverage.
- Take a data set from a production system and "scrub" or anonymize it to remove any personal information while still maintaining the internal integrity of that data. The scrubbed data can then be used for testing without the risk of a security leak or misuse of personal information. This is particularly important where large volumes of realistic data are required, and where security and data privacy risks apply.
- Generate synthetic test data from given sets of input parameters (e.g., for use in random testing). Some of these tools will analyze the database structure to determine what inputs will be required from the Test Analyst.

6.3.3 Automated Test Execution Tools

Test execution tools are used by Test Analysts at all test levels to run automated tests and check the actual results. The objective of using a test execution tool is typically one or more of the following:
- To reduce costs (in terms of effort and/or time)
- To run more tests
- To run the same test in many environments
- To make test execution more repeatable
- To run tests that would be impossible to run manually (i.e., large data validation tests) These

objectives often overlap into the main objectives of increasing coverage while reducing costs.

The return on investment for test execution tools is usually highest when automating regression tests because of the low level of maintenance expected and the repeated execution of the tests. Automating smoke tests can also be an effective use of automation due to the frequent use of the tests, the need for a quick test result and, although the maintenance cost may be higher, the ability to have an automated way to evaluate a new build in a continuous integration environment.

Test execution tools are commonly used during system and integration testing. Some tools, particularly API test tools, may also be used in component testing. Leveraging the tools where they are most applicable will help to improve the return on investment.

7. References

7.1 Standards

[ISO25010]   ISO/IEC 25010 (2011) Systems and software engineering – Systems and software Quality Requirements and Evaluation (SQuaRE) System and software quality models, Chapter 4

[ISO29119-4]   ISO/IEC/IEEE 29119-4 Software and Systems Engineering – Software Testing – Part 4, Test Techniques, 2015

[OMG-DMN]   Object Management Group: OMG® Decision Model and Notation™, Version 1.3, December 2019; url: www.omg.org/spec/DMN/, Chapter 8

[OMG-UML]   Object Management Group: OMG® Unified Modeling Language®, Version 2.5.1, December 2017; url: www.omg.org/spec/UML/

[RTCA DO-178C/ED-12C]   Software Considerations in Airborne Systems and Equipment Certification, RTCA/EUROCAE ED12C, 2013., Chapter 1

7.2 ISTQB® and IREB Documents

[IREB_CPRE]   IREB Certified Professional for Requirements Engineering Foundation Level Syllabus, Version 2.2.2, 2017

[ISTQB_AL_OVIEW]   ISTQB® Advanced Level Overview, Version 2.0

[ISTQB_ALTTA_SYL]   ISTQB® Advanced Level Technical Test Analyst Syllabus, Version 2019

[ISTQB_FL_SYL]   ISTQB® Foundation Level Syllabus, Version 2018

[ISTQB_GLOSSARY]   Standard glossary of terms used in Software Testing, url: https://glossary.istqb.org/

[ISTQB_TAE_SYL]   ISTQB® Advanced Level Test Automation Engineer Syllabus, Version 2017

[ISTQB_UT_SYL]   ISTQB® Foundation Level Specialist Syllabus Usability Testing, Version 2018

7.3 Books and Articles

[Bath14]   Graham Bath, Judy McKay, "The Software Test Engineer's Handbook (2nd Edition)", Rocky Nook, 2014, ISBN 978-1-933952-24-6

[Beizer95]   Boris Beizer, "Black-box Testing", John Wiley & Sons, 1995, ISBN 0-471-12094-4

[Black02]   Rex Black, "Managing the Testing Process (2nd edition)", John Wiley & Sons: New York, 2002, ISBN 0-471-22398-0

[Black07]   Rex Black, "Pragmatic software testing: Becoming an effective and efficient test professional", John Wiley and Sons, 2007, ISBN 978-0-470-12790-2

[Black09]   Rex Black, "Advanced Software Testing, Volume 1", Rocky Nook, 2009, ISBN 978-1-933-952-19-2

[Buwalda02]   Hans Buwalda, "Integrated Test Design and Automation: Using the Test Frame Method", Addison-Wesley Longman, 2002, ISBN 0-201-73725-6

[Chow1978]   T.S. Chow, Testing Software Design Modeled by Finite-State Machines, IEEE Transactions on Software Engineering vol. SE-4, issue 3, May 1978, pp. 178-187

[Cohn04]   Mike Cohn, "User Stories Applied: For Agile Software Development", Addison-Wesley Professional, 2004, ISBN 0-321-20568-5

[Copeland04] Lee Copeland, "A Practitioner's Guide to Software Test Design", Artech House, 2004, ISBN 1-58053-791-X

[Craig02]   Rick David Craig, Stefan P. Jaskiel, "Systematic Software Testing", Artech House, 2002, ISBN 1-580-53508-9

[Forgács19]   István Forgács, Attila Kovács, "Practical Test Design", BCS, 2019, ISBN 978-1-780-1747-23

[Gilb93]   Tom Gilb, Dorothy Graham, "Software Inspection", Addison-Wesley, 1993, ISBN 0-201-63181-4

[Koomen06]   Tim Koomen, Leo van der Aalst, Bart Broekman, Michiel Vroon "TMap NEXT, for result driven testing", UTN Publishers, 2006, ISBN 90-72194-80-2

[Kuhn16]   Richard Kuhn et al, "Introduction to Combinatorial Testing", CRC Press, 2016, ISBN 978-0-429-18515-1

[Mosley93]   Daniel J. Mosley, The Handbook of MIS Application Software Testing, Yourdon Press, Prentice-Hall. 1993, ISBN 978-0-13-907007-5

[Myers11]   Glenford J. Myers, "The Art of Software Testing" 3rd Edition, John Wiley & Sons, 2011, ISBN: 978-1-118-03196-4

[Offutt16]   Jeff Offutt, Paul Ammann, Introduction to Software Testing" 2nd Edition, Cambridge University Press, 2016, ISBN 13: 978-1-107-17201-2,

[vanVeenendaal12]   Erik van Veenendaal, "Practical risk-based testing." Product Risk Management: The PRISMA Method", UTN Publishers, 2012, ISBN 978-94-9098-607-0

[Wiegers03]   Karl Wiegers, "Software Requirements 2", Microsoft Press, 2003, ISBN 0-735-61879-8

[Whittaker03] James Whittaker, "How to Break Software", Addison-Wesley, 2003, ISBN 0-201-79619-8

[Whittaker09]   James Whittaker, "Exploratory software testing: tips, tricks, tours, and techniques to guide test design", Addison-Wesley, 2009, ISBN 0-321-63641-4

7.4 Other References

The following references point to information available on the Internet and elsewhere. Even though these references were checked at the time of publication of this Advanced Level syllabus, the ISTQB® cannot be held responsible if the references are not available anymore.

- Chapter 3
    - Czerwonka, Jacek: www.pairwise.org
    - Defect taxonomy: www.testingeducation.org/a/bsct2.pdf
    - Sample defect taxonomy based on Boris Beizer's work: inet.uni2.dk/~vinter/bugtaxst.doc
    - Good overview of various taxonomies: testingeducation.org/a/bugtax.pdf
    - Heuristic Risk-Based Testing By James Bach
    - Exploring Exploratory Testing, Cem Kaner and Andy Tinkham,
        www.kaner.com/pdfs/ExploringExploratoryTesting.pdf
    - Pettichord, Bret, "An Exploratory Testing Workshop Report",
        www.testingcraft.com/exploratorypettichord
- Chapter 5
    http://www.tmap.net/checklists-and-templates

8. Appendix A

The following table is derived from the complete table provided in ISO 25010. It focusses only on the quality characteristics covered in the Test Analyst syllabus, and compares the terms used in ISO 9126 (as used in the 2012 version of the syllabus) with those in the newer ISO 25010 (as used in this version).

ISO/IEC 25010	ISO/IEC 9126-1	Notes
Functional suitability	**Functionality**	
Functional completeness		
Functional correctness	Accuracy	
Functional appropriateness	Suitability	
	Interoperability	Moved to Compatibility
Usability		
Appropriateness recognizability	Understandability	New name
Learnability	Learnability	
Operability	Operability	
User error protection		New subcharacteristic
User interface aesthetics	Attractiveness	New name
Accessibility		New subcharacteristic
Compatibility		New definition
Interoperability		
Co-Existence		Covered in Technical Test Analyst

9. Index

0-switch, 29
accessibility, 39
accuracy testing, 41
action words, 51
activities, 11
adaptability testing, 45
Agile software development, 12, 13, 48
anonymize, 52
applying the best technique, 38
black-box test technique, 23
black-box test- techniques, 24
boundary value analysis, 23, 26
breadth-first, 22
checklist-based reviewing, 47
checklist-based testing, 23, 35
checklists in reviews, 47
classification tree, 23, 30, 31
combinatorial techniques, 25
combining techniques, 33
compatibility, 39
decision table, 23, 27
defect taxonomy, 23
defect-based test technique, 23, 37
depth-first, 22
equivalence partitioning, 23, 24
error guessing, 23, 34
exit criteria, 10
experience-based test technique, 23
experience-based test techniques, 18, 33, 34, 38
experience-based testing, 23
exploratory testing, 23, 36
functional appropriateness, 39
functional appropriateness testing, 41
functional completeness, 39
functional completeness testing, 41
functional correctness, 39
functional correctness testing, 41
functional suitability, 39
heuristic, 44
high-level test case, 10, 13, 15
installability, 45
interoperability, 39
interoperability testing, 42
ISO 9126, 40
keywords, 51
learnability, 39
low-level test case, 10, 13, 14
N-switch, 29
N-switch coverage, 29
operability, 39
pairwise testing, 23, 31, 32, 42
portability testing, 44
product risk, 13, 19
quality characteristics, 40
quality sub-characteristics, 40
replaceability testing, 45
requirements-based testing, 23
risk assessment, 20
risk identification, 19, 20
risk impact, 21
risk level, 20
risk likelihood, 21
risk mitigation, 19, 21
risk-based test strategy, 17
risk-based testing, 19
SDLC, 11
    Agile, 12, 16
    incremental, 11
    iterative, 11
    sequential, 11, 36
software development lifecycle, 11
standards
    DO-178C, 17
    ED-12C, 17
    ISO 25010, 16, 57
    OMG-DMN, 27
    OMG-UML, 32
state transition testing, 23, 28
suitability, 39
suitability testing, 41
SUMI, 39, 44
test, 10
test analysis, 10, 12
test basis, 15
test case, 15
test charter, 18, 23, 36
test condition, 10, 13
test data, 10
test data preparation tool, 52
test design, 10, 13
test design tool, 52
test environment, 17
test execution, 10, 18
test execution schedule, 10
test execution tool, 52
test implementation, 10, 16
test oracle, 15
test procedure specification, 10
test script, 14

test strategy, 13
test suite, 10, 17
test technique, 23
testing software quality characteristics, 39
unscripted testing, 18
untestable, 47
usability, 39
usability testing, 42
use case testing, 23, 32
user error protection, 39
User error protection, 39
user experience, 39
    evaluation, 43
user interface aesthetics, 39
user stories, 48
user story testing, 23
WAMMI, 39, 44

Sample Exam – Questions
Sample Exam set A
Version 2.6

ISTQB® Test Analyst Syllabus Advanced Level
Compatible with Syllabus version 3.1

International Software Testing Qualifications Board

Version 2.6

Released September 29, 2021

Test Analyst, Advanced Level
Sample Exam set A
Sample Exam – Questions

Copyright Notice

Copyright Notice © International Software Testing Qualifications Board (hereinafter called ISTQB®).

ISTQB® is a registered trademark of the International Software Testing Qualifications Board. All

rights reserved.

The authors hereby transfer the copyright to the ISTQB®. The authors (as current copyright holders) and ISTQB® (as the future copyright holder) have agreed to the following conditions of use:

Extracts, for non-commercial use, from this document may be copied if the source is acknowledged.

Any Accredited Training Provider may use this sample exam in their training course if the authors and the ISTQB® are acknowledged as the source and copyright owners of the sample exam and provided that any advertisement of such a training course is done only after official Accreditation of the training materials has been received from an ISTQB®-recognized Member Board.

Any individual or group of individuals may use this sample exam in articles and books, if the authors and the ISTQB® are acknowledged as the source and copyright owners of the sample exam.

Any other use of this sample exam is prohibited without first obtaining the approval in writing of the ISTQB®.

Any ISTQB®-recognized Member Board may translate this sample exam provided they reproduce the abovementioned Copyright Notice in the translated version of the sample exam.

Document Responsibility

The ISTQB® Examination Working Group is responsible for this document.

Acknowledgements

This document was produced by a core team from ISTQB®: Andreas Gunther, Daniel Poľan, Jean-Baptiste Crouigneau, Lucjan Stapp, Michael Stahl, and Stuart Reid

The core team thanks the Exam Working Group review team, the Syllabus Working Group and the National Boards for their suggestions and input.

This document is maintained by a core team from ISTQB® consisting of the Syllabus Working Group and Exam Working Group.

Test Analyst, Advanced Level
Sample Exam set A
Sample Exam – Questions

Revision History

| Sample Exam – Questions Layout Template used: | Version 2.5 | Date: Maj 21, 2021 |

Version	Date	Remarks
2.6	Sept 29, 2021	Updated the purpose of document Correction to questions: #4, #5, #7, #8, #9, #10, #11, and #13
2.5	May 28, 2021	Update of Table of Context
2.4	May 21, 2021	Update of Copyright Notice Minor correction to Additional question: #1
2.3	March 3, 2021	Updated according to CTAL-TA v3.1.0 update Questions 10 and 11 replaced according to the changed Syllabus contents Updates to the majority of the questions
2.2	Unpublished	New template applied
2.1	December 19, 2019	Revisions made by AELWG to enable launch
2.0	October 5, 2019	Release of sample exam for CTAL-TA 2019
1.3	February 19, 2019	Minor correction of answer option labels Correcting of Pick-N type questions
1.2	December 5, 2018	Split of document into Questions and Answers Randomize answer order Refactor layout on Sample Exam Template Correcting of Pick-N type questions Correcting of question 16 and 17 Remove broken question 15 (and renumbering)
1.01	November 23, 2012	Version for release
1.00	October 19, 2012	Version for voting

Test Analyst, Advanced Level
Sample Exam set A
Sample Exam – Questions

Table of Contents

Copyright Notice 2
Document Responsibility 2
Acknowledgements 2
Revision History 3
Table of Contents 4
Introduction 5
   Purpose of this document 5
   Instructions 5
Questions 6
      Question #1 (1 Point) 6
      Question #2 (1 Point) 6
      Question #3 (1 Point) 6
      Question #4 (3 Points) 7
      Question #5 (3 Point) 8
      Question #6 (1 Point) 9
      Question #7 (2 Points) 10
      Question #8 (3 Points) 11
      Question #9 (3 Points) 12
      Question #10 (3 Points) 13
      Question #11 (3 Points) 14
      Question #13 (3 Points) 16
      Question #14 (1 Point) 17
      Question #15 (3 Points) 17
      Question #16 (3 Points) 18
      Question #17 (3 Points) 19
      Question #18 (3 Points) 20
      Question #19 (3 Points) 21
      Question #20 (3 Points) 22
      Question #21 (1 Point) 22
      Question #22 (2 Points) 23
      Question #23 (1 Point) 23
      Question #24 (3 Points) 24
      Question #25 (1 Point) 25
      Question #26 (1 Point) 25
      Question #27 (1 Point) 26
      Question #28 (1 Point) 26
      Question #29 (1 Point) 26
      Question #30 (1 Point) 27
      Question #31 (1 Point) 27
      Question #32 (1 Point) 28
      Question #33 (1 Point) 28
      Question #34 (3 Points) 29
      Question #35 (3 Points) 30
      Question #36 (2 Points) 31
      Question #37 (2 Points) 32
      Question #38 (2 Points) 33
      Question #39 (2 Points) 34
      Question #40 (1 Point) 34

Test Analyst, Advanced Level
Sample Exam set A
Sample Exam – Questions

Appendix: Additional Questions 35
    Question #1 (1 Point) 35
    Question #2 (1 Point) 35

Introduction

Purpose of this document

The example questions and answers and associated justifications in this sample exam have been created by a team of subject matter experts and experienced question writers with the aim of:

- Assisting ISTQB® Member Boards and Exam Boards in their question writing activities
- Providing training providers and exam candidates with examples of exam questions

These questions cannot be used as-is in any official examination.

Note, that real exams may include a wide variety of questions, and this sample exam *is not* intended to include examples of all possible question types, styles or lengths, also this sample exam may both be more difficult or less difficult than any official exam.

Instructions

In this document you may find:

- Questions[1], including for each question:
  - Any scenario needed by the question stem
  - Point value
  - Response (answer) option set
- Additional questions, including for each question [does not apply to all sample exams]:
  - Any scenario needed by the question stem
  - Point value
  - Response (answer) option set

- *Answers, including justification are contained in a separate document*

---

[1] In this sample exam the questions are sorted by the LO they target; this cannot be expected of a live exam.

Questions

Question #1 (1 Point)
Which of the following statements is TRUE with respect to when the test analyst should become involved during different software development lifecycle models?

  a) In sequential V-model projects the test analyst should start test analysis concurrently with coding
  b) In sequential V-model projects the test analyst should start test analysis concurrently with requirement specification
  c) There are no differences in the moment of involvement for test analysts for the various software development lifecycles
  d) In Agile software development the test analyst should start test analysis and design concurrently with coding

Select ONE option.

Question #2 (1 Point)
Which of the following answers describes the most appropriate and complete set of activities for the Test Analyst to focus on during test analysis and design?

  a) Analyze the test basis, select test techniques, create high-level test conditions for risk mitigation, create test cases to achieve desired coverage of the test basis, create risk mitigation test cases
  b) Analyze risks, create test conditions to address risks, create high-level test cases to meet test conditions for risk mitigation, create all low-level test cases
  c) Select test techniques, create high-level test cases to meet test conditions, create high-level test cases to mitigate risks, create low level tests cases to achieve desired coverage
  d) Analyze the test basis, identify test conditions at appropriate levels to address the test basis, add test conditions for risk mitigation, select test techniques to achieve desired coverage, design test cases

Select ONE option.

Question #3 (1 Point)
Which of the following statements does NOT give a good reason why test cases should be reviewed and understood by stakeholders?

  a) Customer and users review the test cases in order to verify them against requirements, business processes and business rules
  b) The test manager reviews the test cases in order to control the work of the test analyst and to create the organization's test strategy
  c) Testers review test cases written by other testers in order to ensure that the test cases are consistent, understandable and executable by testers other than the author
  d) Developers review test cases written by testers in order to align their understanding of requirements with the testers' and to align component testing with system testing

Select ONE option.

Question #4 (3 Points)

The insurance company SecureLife has started a project IQ (Improved Quality) to implement a new health insurance application. The intention is to make it possible to create online transactions for health insurance claims raised by employees and members of companies or associations having health insurance agreements.

The project team for IQ have testers who are business users with lots of domain knowledge but without much formal test training.

At the same time another project, HIPPOS (Health Insurance Product Public Order Sales), has been started by the marketing department of SecureLife with the purpose of launching a new Internet application that will allow potential buyers of health insurance to use a calculator to calculate insurance premiums.

The new project HIPPOS application will be developed and tested by a team, which have worked together with the marketing department for the last three years, developing marketing web applications. The team consists of well-trained testers and developers. They have implemented test automation for regression testing, and they have checklists of common defects and common security problems which they use in their retrospectives.

As senior Test Analyst in SecureLife you are responsible for designing test cases that achieve high levels of coverage. You need to decide the level of detail and documentation required for test cases in the two projects.

Which of the following are the BEST options?

a) In project HIPPOS the test cases should be written at a high level allowing the testers flexibility in varying the details to achieve higher coverage
b) In project IQ the test cases should be written at a high level. The testers are business users and they know their business rules and calculations so no need for detailed documentation
c) In both project IQ and HIPPOS the test cases should be written as low-level test cases, with thorough documentation and detailed procedures
d) In project IQ the test cases should be written at a low level with documented procedures and traceability to requirements
e) In project HIPPOS the test cases should be written at a low level with documented procedures and audit trails

Select TWO options.

Question #5 (3 Point)
An e-commerce company has started a project to implement an electronic trading platform that allows traders a direct access to Fixed Income OTC (over-the-counter) markets, called B-OTC.

Using B-OTC, traders will be able to submit orders online to these markets to get a faster order execution. B-OTC will process an order through different phases:

- A validation phase of the order
- A price determination phase where several markets are examined looking for the best price
- An execution phase where the order is completed

Which of the following is LEAST likely to influence the decision to design low-level or high-level test cases?

a) The requirements specification for B-OTC is very clear, detailed and exhaustive
b) B-OTC must be compliant to several regulations and an audit of the tests is mandatory
c) The testers are domain experts without specific knowledge of formal testing
d) The sequence of phases an online order will pass through

Select ONE option.

Question #6 (1 Point)
Which of the following statements is INCORRECT regarding test implementation activities?

a) Test Analysts may create data to be used with keyword-driven test automation
b) If a risk-based test strategy is being used, risk priority order may dictate the execution order for the test cases
c) When creating the test execution schedule, manual and automated test execution are considered to be independent activities
d) Test Analysts must verify the procedures that gather data for evaluating current status against exit criteria

Select ONE option

Question #7 (2 Points)

A project to develop a foreign exchange Automated Teller Machine for an airport has been planned and a risk assessment has shown that there are three key risks:

- There is a risk that usability will be a problem for visually impaired users because the operation requires viewing several screens in sequence with relatively small text. This has been assessed as medium likelihood with high impact
- There is a risk that response will be relatively slow because the foreign exchange rates will be checked before each transaction; this has been assessed as medium likelihood with medium impact
- There is a risk that accuracy of calculations could lead to cumulative errors. This has been assessed as low likelihood with high impact

The test strategy currently requires performance testing and usability testing during system test, and functional correctness testing at every test level. The project schedule is under time pressure.

Which of the following possible risk mitigation actions should be prioritized highest?

a) Review the calculation algorithms and work with specialists to define a data set for calculation tests
b) Defer usability testing until UAT and recruit visually impaired testers to join the UAT team
c) Involve visually impaired users in the review of the user interface design
d) Spend time with developers to identify operational scenarios to test performance

Select ONE option.

Question #8 (3 Points)

A company has set up an employee wellness program and combined it with the payment for health insurance:

The program has the following rules:

1. Employees who consume 20 units or less of alcohol per week get $30 off their payment
2. Employees who fill in a "health risk assessment" will be rewarded with a $25 reduction in payment
3. Employees who participate in a health control programme at the company:
    1. Receive a $50 reduction in their payment for having a BMI of 27.5 or less, and a $25 reduction for having a BMI below 30
    2. Non-smokers receive an additional $50 reduction in their payment
    3. Smokers who have joined a stop-smoking class receive a $25 reduction
    4. Smokers who have not joined a stop-smoking class pay an additional premium of $75

How many test cases are needed to achieve 100% coverage of equivalence partitions of the valid input parameters, when testing this specification by applying the equivalence partitioning test technique?

a) 3 test cases
b) 4 test cases
c) 5 test cases
d) 12 test cases

Select ONE option.

Question #9 (3 Points)

You are working on a customer loyalty application for a restaurant. Customers earn points by spending money on food. There are four categories for awards that are based on the number of points earned.

- Casual: 1 - 40 points
- Regular: 41 - 150 points
- Frequent: 151 - 300 points
- Elite: more than 300 points

Existing tests cases have already covered the point values 12, 150, 151, 152 and 301.

What is the percentage of boundary value coverage you have already achieved with existing test cases?

a) 37.5%
b) 42.8%
c) 50%
d) 62.5%

Select ONE answer.

Question #10 (3 Points)

The Business Analysts have provided the following specification for the payment options of an internet store:

"A customer must provide credit card details (including expiry date) to the internet store during registration. They can use any of the three payment options: credit card, instant transfer, and direct debit payment. Direct debit is only available for purchase amounts up to 500 €. For non- registered customers, the only allowed payment option is instant transfer."

A Test Analyst has designed the following collapsed decision table that should contain rules for the possible combinations:

ID	Conditions	R1	R2	R3	R4
C1	Registered customer	T	T	T	F
C2	Credit card expired	F	T	-	-
C3	Purchase amount <= 500 €	T	T	F	-
	Actions				
A1	Credit card option offered	Y	N	Y	N
A2	Instant transfer option offered	Y	Y	Y	Y
A3	Direct debit option offered	Y	Y	N	N

You are reviewing the decision table for completeness, correctness, and consistency. Which of the following are CORRECT findings?

a) The table is incomplete because three Boolean conditions require 2^3 = 8 rules
b) The rule R3 is not correct because it potentially offers the credit card option to registered customers whose credit card has expired
c) The value '-' (don't care) for condition C2 in rule R4 should rather be a 'N/A' (not applicable) because the system has no information on credit cards for non-registered customers
d) The value '-' (don't care) for condition C3 in rule R4 is incorrect, because if Amount <= 500€ is 'True', direct debit should be offered
e) The table is inconsistent because for a registered customer with an expired credit card and a purchase amount > 500€ both rules R2 and R3 apply

Select TWO options.

Question #11 (3 Points)

As a Test Analyst, you are testing the download functionality of a mobile application via the cellular network with the decision table testing technique. The specification states:

"Before starting a download, the application verifies that the cellular network connectivity is at least two bars strong and the subscription has sufficient data volume to download the file. In the borderline case of two bars connectivity, a buffer of at least 20 KB additional data volume is needed."

During test analysis, you have designed and successfully reviewed the following decision table:

ID	Conditions	R1	R2	R3	R4	R5
C1	Mobile cellular connection strength	< 2 bars	>= 2 bars	2 bars	2 bars	>= 3 bars
C2	Data volume available	N/A	not enough room	insufficient buffer	sufficient buffer	enough room
	Actions					
A1	Download the file	N	N	N	Y	Y
A2	Message "Insufficient data volume available"	N	Y	N	N	N
A3	Message "Insufficient connectivity"	Y	N	Y	N	N

You are designing a test suite that should cover all five decision rules.

Which of the following statements about a test suite for this specification covering all five rules is CORRECT?

  a) The test cases should have two inputs: mobile cellular connection strength and the difference between the data volume available and the file size
  b) The test data should contain at least two files of different sizes: one greater than or equal to 20 KB and one less than 20 KB
  c) The test suite should contain at least three different test cases with connection strength = 2 bars which cover the three possible expected outcomes respectively: A1, A2, and A3
  d) Any test case with an input consisting of connection strength, data volume available and a file size to be downloaded will cover exactly one rule of the decision table

Select ONE option.

Question #12 (3 Points)

The following state transition diagram describes the behavior of a generic scheduler of an Operating System (OS):

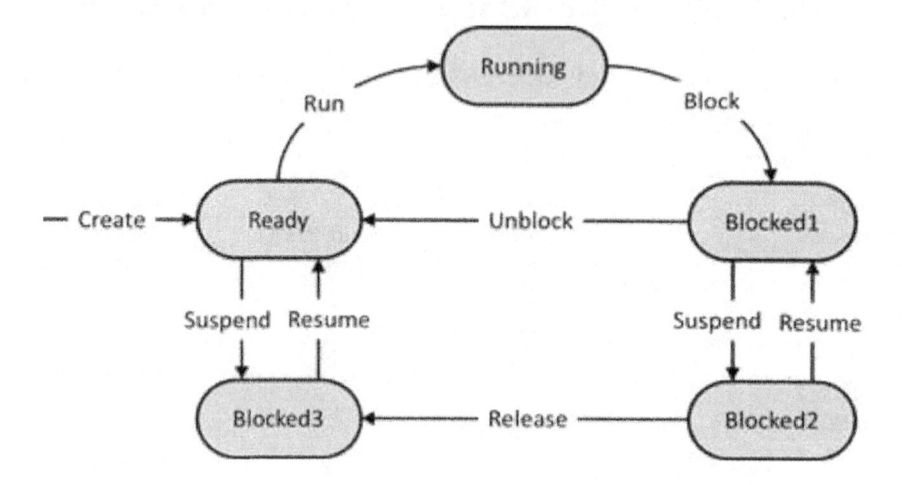

Assume a test always starts in the "Ready" state and ends when the system returns to the "Ready" state, so a test input consists of a sequence ("Ready", event, next state, ..., event, "Ready"), where all states except first and last one is different than "Ready".

What is the MINIMUM number of tests needed to achieve 1-switch coverage?

a) 2
b) 3
c) 4
d) 5

Select ONE answer

Question #13 (3 Points)

A mobile device operates in one of three states: IDLE, STAND-BY, and READY. Its behavior is depicted by the following state transition diagram.

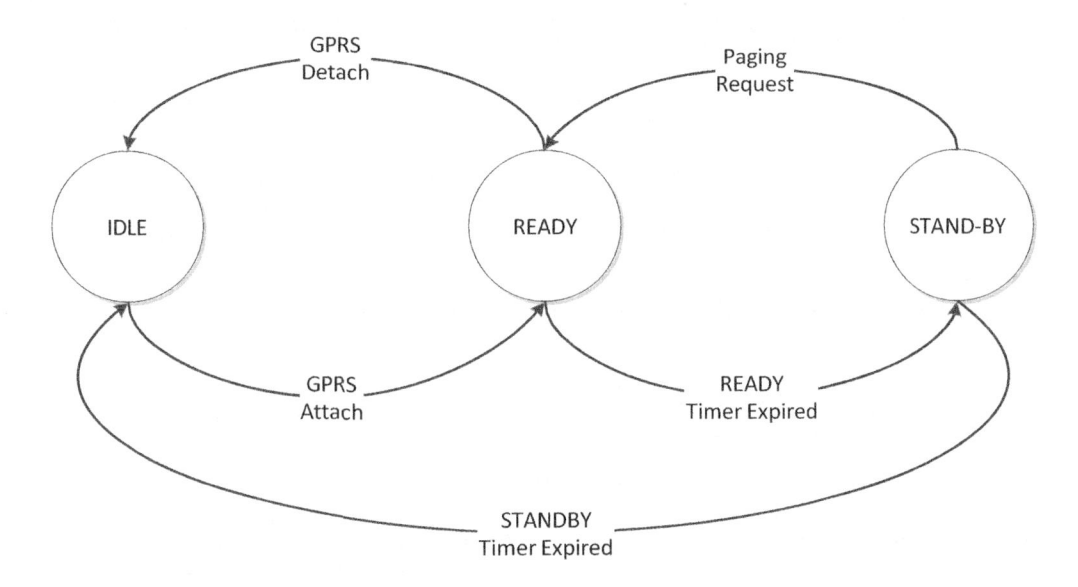

Considering only the READY state, what is the number of test cases required to achieve round-trip coverage for this state?

a) 3
b) 4
c) 6
d) 7

Select ONE option.

Question #14 (1 Point)
Which of the following statements does NOT describe the use of classification trees to support black-box test techniques?

    a) Classification trees support the identification of equivalence partitions
    b) Classification trees support the identification of boundary values
    c) Classification trees support the identification of rules to be used in a decision table
    d) Classification trees support pairwise testing

Select ONE option.

Question #15 (3 Points)
A company offering house insurance policies has several policy options. They depend on the following factors:

    Building type: house, semi-detached, apartment building, cottage Material: wood, concrete, brick, mixed
    Location: city, suburb, countryside, wilderness

You are testing the system and using the pairwise technique for creating test cases.

Using the pairwise technique, how many test cases are required to achieve all pairs coverage?

    a) 16
    b) 12
    c) 64
    d) 4

Select ONE option.

Test Analyst, Advanced Level
Sample Exam set A
Sample Exam – Questions

Question #16 (3 Points)

Consider a multi-language web application with the following requirements:

- Support three different languages: English, French and Japanese
- Run on three different browsers: Br1, Br2, Br3
- Run on three different operating systems: OpS1, OpS2 and OpS3

You have been asked to test the correct behavior of this application for various combinations of languages, browsers and operating systems.

Due to the restricted amount of time you decide to apply the pairwise test technique for creating test cases.

Using the pairwise technique, what is the MINIMUM number of test cases needed to achieve all-pairs coverage?

a) 3
b) 6
c) 9
d) 27

Select ONE option.

Question #17 (3 Points)

Easytravel is a card which is used to paying for journeys on buses and subways. The user can store credit to the card at the Easytravel Loading Machines and the system automatically deducts the journey fee when the user inserts the card into the card reader/writer on a bus or at the subway station. You are a member of the Easytravel project team, and the following user story has been given to you for reviewing.

USE CASE: ADD TO EASYTRAVEL BALANCE FROM CREDIT CARD
Use case ID: UC-201201
Purpose: User is increasing the balance on their Easytravel card Actors: user, system
Pre-conditions: User has a valid Easytravel card and a credit card

Main behavior

User	System
1. User inserts the Easytravel card into the card reader/writer of the Easytravel Loading Machine	2. The system asks what the user wishes to do: (Exception E1) • Query card balance (⇨ separate use case) • Add to balance of the card • Check latest card transactions (⇨ separate use case)
3. User chooses "Add balance"	4. System asks the amount. (Exception E1)
5. User selects the amount	6. System asks for the payment method: (Exception E1) • Cash (⇨ separate use case) • Credit card
7. User selects credit card	8. System asks the user to insert credit card into the credit card reader (Exception E1)
9. User inserts the credit card	10. System shows the amount to be charged from the credit card and asks for confirmation (Exception E2)
11. User confirms the amount	12. System makes the credit card transaction and adds the amount to the Easytravel card balance
13. User removes the credit card and the Easytravel card	14. System prints out a receipt of the transaction
	15. System returns to the main screen

Exceptions

Exception	Action
E1	User can stop the process by removing the Easytravel card from the card reader/writer
E2	If the user does not accept the amount to be charged, he; can cancel the operation by pressing the Cancel button on the credit card reader

End-result: User's Easytravel card balance has been increased with the selected amount and the equal amount has been charged to the credit card.

How many test cases are required to achieve the minimum coverage for this use case?

a) 2 test cases b) 1 test case
c) 9 test cases d) 6 test cases Select ONE option.

Question #18 (3 Points)

TS is a skills portal which is made available to all IT professionals. Individual IT professionals first discuss their training needs with their manager and as a result may receive a voucher from the manager for any of the course types provided at the company. The IT professional uses TS and their voucher to select a specific course and make a reservation.

USE CASE: COURSE REGISTATION Use
Case ID: UC-15504
Purpose: Enable IT professionals to select and reserve a course for which they have been given a voucher
Actors: IT Professional (ITP); TS Skills Portal (SP)
Pre-conditions: none

Main behavior

Step	Action
1	The ITP launches SP
2	SP displays its home page and requests a voucher code from the ITP
3	The ITP enters the voucher code (Exception E1)
4	SP lists the dates, locations and current number of registered participants for the course indicated in the voucher code. (Exception E2)
5	The ITP selects a date and location
6	SP shows an overview of the selected course's contents
7	The ITP confirms selection of this course by pressing the "Register" button
8	SP places the ITP onto the list of participants and a message shown "You are registered for the course"
9	The ITP logs out

Alternative behavior steps

Step	Action
3a	The ITP may log out from the application's home page
8a	If the course already has 12 participants SP places the ITP onto a waiting list and a message shown "you are on the waiting list". SP updates the waiting list

Exceptions

Exception	Action
E1	If an invalid voucher code is entered, SP shows a message "Voucher not known – please try again" is issued. SP returns to the home page (step 2)
E2	If no courses are available SP shows a message "sorry- no courses available – please log out and talk to your manager ". SP returns to the home page (step 2)

How many test cases are required to achieve the minimum coverage for this use case?

a) 1
b) 2
c) 4   d) 3

Select ONE option.

Question #19 (3 Points)

A new mobile app is to be developed for managing the membership of a soccer club which runs several teams. One of the key objectives of the club owners is to replace the outdated manual method required for registration of new members. The functionality of the app is to remain relatively simple because not all users will be familiar with modern user interfaces. The club owners have therefore placed emphasis on the ease with which users can navigate between the various screens and the usability of the application. An objective is also to manage the numbers of players who can register for a team. Limits are therefore to be enforced which may result in applicants being placed on a waiting list.

Which TWO of the following test techniques would be MOST appropriate for testing the mobile app?

a) State transition testing
b) Decision table testing
c) Boundary value analysis
d) Use case testing
e) Pairwise testing

Select TWO options.

Test Analyst, Advanced Level
Sample Exam set A
Sample Exam – Questions

Question #20 (3 Points)

A system is being specified for use by automotive dealers. The system will provide the ability to configure a vehicle's optional characteristics (e.g., engine size, external trim, color), visualize the configured vehicle and generate the retail price of the vehicle. An existing system can provide a visual model of any single configuration, but it does not enable the user to modify the configuration in the same session. This system is being used as a development prototype from which it is expected that the required functionality can be generated more quickly than working from scratch, and time scales have been adjusted for a rapid delivery.

Which of the following test techniques would together give the best chance of achieving acceptable coverage in the available time frame?

  a) State transition testing
  b) Classification tree
  c) Boundary value analysis
  d) Use case testing
  e) Equivalence partitioning

Select TWO options.

Question #21 (1 Point)

Which of the following statements BEST explains experience-based testing?

  a) If the testers are experienced and have good knowledge of the system under test, experience-based techniques are a viable alternative to more formal techniques if there are problems with the quality of the documentation or if the project is under a tight schedule
  b) Experience-based techniques should generally be used if there are no suitable formal techniques or if it takes too much time and effort to use them
  c) Experience-based techniques rely on the tester's knowledge and experience and can therefore be used to increase the coverage as the tester knows which areas need more testing
  d) If checklists are used, experience-based testing can be more systematic and efficient and can replace black-box test techniques

Select ONE option.

Question #22 (2 Points)

You are a Test Analyst on a new project. The requirements documents are on a very high level, containing little detail about the problem the software should address. As a result, your manager has decided that exploratory testing will be a primary test technique used for this project. You have been given the task of specifying, executing, and recording the test sessions.

Which of the options below define what you will need or will use for these tasks?

a) Use debriefing sessions with the test manager or a test lead to record the results of the test sessions
b) Log defects into the defect management system but do not record a pass/fail for the exploratory session because duplicating the results could be difficult
c) Ask end users to execute some ad-hoc testing and note down their actions for future use as exploratory sessions
d) Procure domain knowledge to be applied during the exploratory session
e) Record the results in email and send the email to the test manager and test lead

Select TWO options.

Question #23 (1 Point)

Which of the following describes typical characteristics of defect-based test techniques?

a) Defect-based techniques are based on the analysis and classification of previously found defects
b) Defect-based techniques are mainly used at the component test level
c) Defect-based techniques concentrate on defects found during the analysis of the documentation of a system
d) Defect-based techniques are a sub-category of black-box test techniques

Select ONE option.

Question #24 (3 Points)

The marketing department of insurance company, SecureLife, has started a project called HIPPOS (Health Insurance Product Public Order Sales). The purpose of the project is to create a new Internet application where potential customers can calculate insurance premiums and bonuses based on age and different health factors.

The new application will also make it possible for individual customers to order health insurance products online.

The new application created by project HIPPOS will be developed and tested by SecureLife's Agile development team. The Agile development team has worked together and with the marketing team for the last three years, developing web applications. The Agile team consists of well-trained testers and developers. They have implemented test automation for configuration and regression testing, and they have built taxonomies of common defects and common security problems.

In Project HIPPOS the Product Owner from Marketing has presented the following user stories to the Agile team before the first release planning meeting.

> US1: The Web health insurance calculator shall calculate insurance premiums and bonuses according to the rules described by the actuary and insurance calculation business section
> US2: The user interface of the HIPPOS application shall follow the same standards as the other marketing web applications and use a predefined setup of page frames and dialogs that have been used for the last two years
> US3: The Web applications shall support the latest 3 versions of different types of web browsers Internet Explorer, Google Chrome, Firefox, and Safari
> US4: Security must be at the same level as for other marketing web applications

The Agile team has been asked to prepare a test approach. The Product Owner asks the team to present their proposal for the use of test techniques at the release planning meeting.

Which of the following proposals best supports the given scenario?

a) The Agile team will use exploratory testing as the primary test technique. For user story US1 equivalence partitioning and boundary value analysis will also be used, and an additional black-box test technique will be used for user story US4
b) The Agile team will use exploratory testing and defect-based testing as the primary test techniques. For user story US1 decision table testing will also be used. Adaptability testing for user story US3 and attack-based testing using a checklist will be used extra for user story US4
c) The Agile team will use exploratory testing as the primary test technique. For user story US1 interoperability testing will also be used. Adaptability testing will be used for user story US3 and attack-based testing will also be used for user story US4
d) The Agile team will use black-box test techniques as the primary test techniques. For user story US1 state transition testing and boundary value analysis will also be used, and exploratory testing will also be used in addition for user story US4

Select ONE option.

Question #25 (1 Point)

You are working on a project testing a new application that handles foreign currency exchange transactions. Much of the software which handles calculations and money transfers has been re-used from a similar application which has been used for over 3 years. Several new functions are to be added to the new application to improve the user experience and display graphical information better. The users have not been fully involved in the definition of these new aspects and new functions have therefore been implemented according to the developer's expectations.

As a Test Analyst, which of the following quality characteristics would you focus the MOST on when testing the new application?

a) Functional correctness
b) Functional completeness
c) Replaceability
d) Recoverability

Select ONE option.

Question #26 (1 Point)

You work in Agile software development in the telecommunications industry. The application offers a new interface to allow customers to modify their mobile phone plan directly via the web application. You are performing system tests and work particularly on the screen used to change the mobile phone plan.

The user story you are testing is:

> US-34: As a customer, I want to be able to select a new mobile phone plan online so that I can adapt it to my needs.

As part of these tests, you and the product owner invite a business expert to perform an exploratory test on this screen and indicate if they have any comments on whether the proposed solution allows them to make all the possible changes.

What kind of test are you performing?

a) Functional correctness testing
b) Accessibility testing
c) Adaptability testing
d) Functional appropriateness testing

Select ONE option.

Question #27 (1 Point)
Which of the following statements is correct regarding quality sub-characteristics and the defects they target?

a) Functional completeness testing discovers indications that the system will not be able to meet the needs of the user in a way that will be considered acceptable
b) Functional reliability testing ensures that the functions are available when called
c) Functional appropriateness may focus on the coverage of high-level business cases by the implemented functionality
d) Functional correctness testing involves detecting incorrect handling of data or situations

Select ONE option.

Question #28 (1 Point)
Assume you work for a company that has developed software to help users trade currencies. A new version of the software is being developed. The main feature of this version is the ability to calculate different amounts of commission depending on the volume of the trades. In addition, different categories of users (beginner, intermediate, expert) are defined, and different functions are provided to them according to their category.

You are the Test Analyst responsible for creating functional suitability tests.

Which of the following statements correctly defines the level in the software development lifecycle at which functional suitability tests should be performed earliest?

a) Testing that commissions have been calculated correctly for low-volume trades should be performed during component testing
b) Testing the appropriateness of functions assigned to different user categories should be performed during acceptance testing
c) The interoperability of the new functions with other trading systems should be conducted in system testing
d) Testing that commissions have been calculated correctly for high-volume trades should be performed during system testing
e) Required coverage of high-level business processes should be determined for system integration testing

Select TWO options.

Question #29 (1 Point)
When is functional appropriateness testing usually conducted?

a) During component and integration testing
b) During integration and system testing
c) During system and user acceptance testing
d) During acceptance testing, especially alpha and beta testing

Select ONE answer

Question #30 (1 Point)
Which of the following statements is correct regarding usability testing?

a) The usability should be verified against the requirements and validated by the real users
b) Validation of the usability requirements should be done after release to enable real users to participate
c) Heuristic evaluation can be used to survey the users and find usability problems
d) Usability can be verified by running a comparison with the existing unacceptable product

Select ONE option.

Question #31 (1 Point)
Assume you work for a company that has developed a software component to help users securely and easily manage all the passwords they have defined for different websites. This component is integrated into hundreds of websites, used by millions of people world-wide.

A new software version of the component is being developed. The main feature of this version is the integration with a specific operating system that does not currently support this component.

Which of the following does not qualify as an interoperability failure?

a) Passwords are not saved for all websites which integrate with the component
b) 5% of the websites do not run on a specific operating system
c) Passwords are truncated on some browsers
d) Saving the passwords becomes too complicated for some users

Select ONE option.

Question #32 (1 Point)

You work as a Test Analyst in the team developing a system for managing rented electric scooters. The system consists of the following three parts:

1. A client application for mobile phones
2. Scooter monitoring
3. A server application that supervises the work of the whole

The most important target for your team is to ensure the cooperation between modules.

Based on this description only, which quality characteristic is the most important for you, and should be tested first?

a) Usability
b) Interoperability
c) Security
d) Performance

Select ONE answer

Question #33 (1 Point)

Which of the following statements define types of defect you would NOT typically consider in portability testing?

a) An application does not function correctly in all intended target environments
b) Software cannot be installed for particular configurations
c) Users with disabilities cannot interact with the application
d) Certain software components within a system cannot be exchanged for others
e) Incorrect data exchange between interacting components

Select TWO options.

Question #34 (3 Points)

The HeatWell mobile application shall enable homeowners to control and monitor the heating of their home. The following requirements have been identified as the most important for the HeatWell app:

>Requirement 1: The user must be provided with an interface with which they can easily set required heating times and temperatures and monitor the temperature in different parts of the house.

>Requirement 2: An efficiency function shall calculate the energy consumed and help the user to optimize their needs.

You are the Test Analyst on the HeatWell team.

Which of the following test conditions would you consider to be the most appropriate for verifying the functional and/or non-functional quality characteristics of the stated requirements?

a) The user can install the app on an Android device
b) The user can effectively set target temperatures with a minimum number of steps
c) The efficiency function accurately calculates heat consumption
d) Energy consumption data can be saved on the HeatWell database server for iOS and Android devices
e) Monitoring data can be displayed for the previous 30 days

Select TWO options.

Question #35 (3 Points)

You are a Test Analyst working on a brand-new project.

The customer is a state social welfare administration that wants to improve its website. The website will contain information, news, and documentation on social welfare. It will allow any citizen to interact online in order to view their current status as well as ongoing and past reimbursements.

A team of business analysts, requirement engineers and user experience specialists have worked with the client to gather a comprehensive list of the requirements for the new website, based on the existing website, new needs, new best practices, and user feedback.

The project follows the V-model as software development lifecycle.

The requirements have been reviewed and approved by all the stakeholders.

You are now about to start the test design based on requirements and a draft of detailed specifications.

Here is a selection of some requirements:

- R003 – The entire website must be accessible to users with visual disabilities, according to WCAG 2.0
- R004 – The website must work properly on the devices presently utilized by users of the existing website, covering at least 80% of these users
- R005 – The response time of the website must not exceed 5 seconds under the load created by 5.000 simultaneous users
- R006 – The new system must keep all the non-technical data used in the previous system
- R007 – Only the owner and authorized state agents must be able to access personal data in the system

Which of the requirements above should you, according to your responsibilities, consider for your test design?

a) R003, R005, R006
b) R003, R004
c) R003, R004, R007
d) R004, R006, R007

Select ONE option

Question #36 (2 Points)

You are reviewing the following requirements specification document:

Document: Req. spec 101-A	
Object: Transaction screen	
Author: Susie Specifier	Date written: 2019-03-15
Version: 0.23	System: Bookkeeping TA-AB1
Subsystem: 2a15	Use cases applicable to project? Yes
Description:	

Description:

User must be able to browse customer's transactions on the customer's account. It must be possible to view the transactions either chronologically from the oldest to the newest or the opposite way, or by their transaction ID. The field containing the detailed transaction information must be long enough to contain the name of the transaction counterparty (maximum 20 characters), their ID number (6 digits) and the transaction identifier (8 digits).

It must be possible to change between the Transaction screen and User information screen with the "Swap screen" –button.

The layout of the Transaction screen is described in more detail in a separate document.

- The retrieval time of new data must be less than 3 seconds per screen. The number of simultaneous users will vary between 20 and 40 and is expected to increase to 60 within a year
- More details about the performance requirements can be found in a separate performance requirements specification document

The following is the checklist you are using for this review:

1. Is each requirement testable?
2. Does each requirement have acceptance criteria listed?
3. Does each requirement have a defined priority level?
4. Are the requirements uniquely identified?
5. Is the specification versioned?
6. Is there traceability visible from each requirement to the business/marketing requirements?
7. Is there traceability between the requirements and the use cases (if applicable)?

You are reviewing the specification above with the provided checklist. Assume you have access to the document that provides more information about the screen layout. Which of the items on the checklist are NOT met by the specification?

a) 1, 2, 3
b) 4, 6, 7
c) 3, 5, 7 d) 4, 5, 6

Select ONE option

Question #37 (2 Points)

You are a Test Analyst assigned to a project for the development of a new online banking application. You were asked to participate in the requirements review. For your individual preparation you are given a checklist to help you to check basics rules in requirements writing.

The following is one of the requirements:

> R034 – Even a person unfamiliar with software applications must be able to make a bank transfer

The following is an extract of the checklist:

I. The requirement must be testable
II. The requirement must have an identifier
III. The requirement must always show its version number
IV. The requirement must show traceability to one or more business/marketing requirements

Without further information on this requirement. Which of the following four checklist items are correct with respect to the requirement?

a) All the items are respected
b) I and II are respected
c) Only II is respected
d) Only I is respected

Select ONE option

Question #38 (2 Points)

Easytravel is a card which is used to paying for journeys on buses and subways. The user can store credit to the card at the Easytravel Loading Machines and the system automatically deducts the journey fee when the user presents the card to the card reader on a bus or at the subway station.

You are a member of the Easytravel project team, and the following user story has been given to you for reviewing.

> USER STORY: Add credit to the Easytravel card
> Priority: 1

As a bus passenger, I want to add credit to my Easytravel card so that I can pay for bus rides using the card

FEATURE

Action	Acceptance Criteria
User puts the Easytravel card into a card reader on the Easytravel Loading Machine.	The loading machine displays an option to top up funds on the card 's balance.
Loading machine checks card credentials	Card rejected if invalid
User selects "top up card".	Loading machine is ready
User puts in one or more cash notes.	The loading machine shows an increase to the card's balance according to note(s) entered.
Loading machine contacts back-end system with update.	Back-end system is updated
User selects "exit".	User is prompted to remove their Easytravel card.

Consider the following checklist for a good user story. Which of these criteria are NOT achieved regarding this user story?

a) Is the story written entirely from the view of the person who is requesting it?
b) Is the feature clearly defined and distinct?
c) Are the acceptance criteria defined and testable?
d) Is the story prioritized?
e) Does the story follow the commonly used format?

Select TWO options.

Question #39 (2 Points)

A business application is in the maintenance phase and several changes to the business logic have either already been implemented or are expected be implemented in the next release. Test automation is used to ensure that business cases are regression tested whenever a change is made. A keyword-driven approach is used for the test automation. Since the last release, some emergency fixes were necessary, and the test automation reports are now highlighting anomalies.

Which of the following steps should now be conducted by the Test Analyst?

a) Update the keywords and data to reflect changes made
b) Modularize the automation scripts
c) Analyze anomalies to determine if the problem is with the keywords, the input data, the automation script itself or with the application being tested
d) Ask the developer to manually step through the failed automated test with the same data to see if the failure is in the application itself
e) If the cause of the anomaly cannot be found remove the test from the automated regression testing pack

Select TWO options.

Question #40 (1 Point)

Which of the following statements does NOT describe a benefit from using testing tools?

a) Test data preparation tools can "anonymize" data while still maintaining the internal integrity of that data
b) Test execution tools enable fewer tests to be run, which reduces costs and the efficiency of regression tests
c) Test design tools can help the Test Analyst to choose the types of tests that are needed to obtain a targeted level of coverage
d) Test execution tools enable the same tests to be repeated in many environments

Select ONE option.

Appendix: Additional Questions

Question #1 (1 Point)
Which of the following issues should be considered when designing test cases?

    a) The same test basis should be used for different test levels
    b) Expected results may include environmental postconditions
    c) The process may be effective when combined with dynamic analysis
    d) The required detailed test infrastructure requirements should be finalized

Select ONE option.

Question #2 (1 Point)
Which of the following answers describes the most appropriate and complete set of activities for the Test Analyst to focus on during test execution?

    a) Conducting exploratory test sessions, reporting defects, analyzing anomalies, comparing expected and actual results, updating traceability information based on test results
    b) Implementing test automation, finalizing the test environments, analyzing anomalies, reporting defects, comparing expected and actual results
    c) Logging test outcomes, reporting defects, analyzing anomalies, organizing tests into test suites, identifying the test conditions
    d) Analyzing the test basis, performing manual tests, select test case design techniques, analyzing anomalies, updating traceability information based on test results

Select ONE option.

Sample Exam – Answers
Sample Exam set A
Version 2.6

ISTQB® Test Analyst Syllabus
Advanced Level
Compatible with Syllabus version 3.1

International Software Testing Qualifications Board

Version 2.6   Released September 29, 2021

Test Analyst, Advanced Level
Sample Exam set A
Sample Exam – Answers

Copyright Notice

Copyright Notice © International Software Testing Qualifications Board (hereinafter called ISTQB®).

ISTQB® is a registered trademark of the International Software Testing Qualifications Board. All

rights reserved.

The authors hereby transfer the copyright to the ISTQB®. The authors (as current copyright holders) and ISTQB® (as the future copyright holder) have agreed to the following conditions of use:

Extracts, for non-commercial use, from this document may be copied if the source is acknowledged.

Any Accredited Training Provider may use this sample exam in their training course if the authors and the ISTQB® are acknowledged as the source and copyright owners of the sample exam and provided that any advertisement of such a training course is done only after official Accreditation of the training materials has been received from an ISTQB®-recognized Member Board.

Any individual or group of individuals may use this sample exam in articles and books, if the authors and the ISTQB® are acknowledged as the source and copyright owners of the sample exam.

Any other use of this sample exam is prohibited without first obtaining the approval in writing of the ISTQB®.

Any ISTQB®-recognized Member Board may translate this sample exam provided they reproduce the abovementioned Copyright Notice in the translated version of the sample exam.

Document Responsibility

The ISTQB® Examination Working Group is responsible for this document.

Acknowledgements

This document was produced by a core team from the ISTQB®: Andreas Gunther, Daniel Poľan, Jean-Baptiste Crouigneau, Lucjan Stapp, Michael Stahl, and Stuart Reid

The core team thanks the Exam Working Group review team, the Syllabus Working Group and the National Boards for their suggestions and input.

This document is maintained by a core team from ISTQB® consisting of the Syllabus Working Group and Exam Working Group.

Test Analyst, Advanced Level
Sample Exam set A
Sample Exam – Answers

Revision History

Sample Exam – Answers Layout Template used:	Version 2.6	Date: September 29, 2021

Version	Date	Remarks
2.6	September 29, 2021	Updated the purpose of document Correction to answers: #4, #5, #7, #8, #9, #10, #11, #12, and #13
2.5	May 28, 2021	Minor correction to answer: #11, and #13
2.4	May 21, 2021	Update of Copyright Notice Minor correction to answers: #11, #12, #13, #16, #18, #26, and #37
2.3	March 3, 2021	Updated according to CTAL-TA v3.1.0 update Questions 10 and 11 replaced according to the changed Syllabus contents Updates to majority of the answers
2.2	unpublished	New template applied
2.1	December 19, 2019	Revisions made by AELWG to enable launch
2.0	October 5, 2019	Release of sample exam for CTAL-TA 2019
1.3	February 19, 2019	Minor correction of answer option labels Correcting of Pick-N type answers
1.2	December 5, 2018	Split of document into Questions and Answers Randomize answer order Refactor layout on Sample Exam Template Correcting of Pick-N type answers Correcting of answer #16 and #17 Remove broken answer #15 (and renumbering)
1.01	November 23, 2012	Version for release
1.00	October 19, 2012	Version for voting

Table of Contents

Copyright Notice 2
Document Responsibility 2
Acknowledgements 2
Revision History 3
Table of Contents 4
Introduction 5
   Purpose of this document 5
   Instructions 5
Answer Key 6
Answers 7
   1 7
   2 7
   3 7
   4 8
   5 8
   6 9
   7 9
   8 10
   9 11
   10 12
   11 13
   12 14
   13 16
   14 17
   15 18
   16 19
   17 20
   18 21
   19 22
   20 23
   21 24
   22 24
   23 25
   24 26
   25 27
   26 27
   27 27
   28 28
   29 28
   30 29
   31 29
   32 29
   33 29
   34 30
   35 30
   36 31
   37 31
   38 32
   39 32

Test Analyst, Advanced Level
Sample Exam set A
Sample Exam – Answers

40 32
Appendix: Answers to Additional Questions 33
    1 33
    2 33

Introduction

Purpose of this document

The example questions and answers and associated justifications in this sample exam have been created by a team of subject matter experts and experienced question writers with the aim of:

- Assisting ISTQB® Member Boards and Exam Boards in their question writing activities
- Providing training providers and exam candidates with examples of exam questions

These questions cannot be used as-is in any official examination.

Note, that real exams may include a wide variety of questions, and this sample exam *is not* intended to include examples of all possible question types, styles or lengths, also this sample exam may both be more difficult or less difficult than any official exam.

Instructions

In this document you may find:

- Answer Key table, including for each correct answer:
    - K-level, Learning Objective, and Point value
- Answer sets, including for all questions:
    - Correct answer
    - Justification for each response (answer) option
    - K-level, Learning Objective, and Point value
- Additional answer sets, including for all questions [does not apply to all sample exams]:
    - Correct answer
    - Justification for each response (answer) option
    - K-level, Learning Objective, and Point value

- *Questions are contained in a separate document*

Test Analyst, Advanced Level
Sample Exam set A
Sample Exam – Answers

Answer Key

Question Number (#)	Correct Answer	LO	K-Level	Points
1	b	TA-1.2.1	K2	1
2	d	TA-1.3.1	K2	1
3	b	TA-1.4.1	K2	1
4	a, d	TA-1.4.2	K4	3
5	d	TA-1.4.2	K4	1
6	c	TA-1.5.1	K2	1
7	c	TA-2.1.1	K3	2
8	B	TA-3.2.1	K4	3
9	a	TA-3.2.2	K4	3
10	b, c	TA-3.2.3	K4	3
11	d	TA-3.2.3	K4	3
12	c	TA-3.2.4	K4	3
13	a	TA-3.2.4	K4	3
14	c	TA-3.2.5	K2	1
15	a	TA-3.2.6	K4	3
16	c	TA-3.2.6	K4	3
17	d	TA-3.2.7	K4	3
18	c	TA-3.2.7	K4	3
19	a, c	TA-3.2.8	K4	3
20	b, e	TA-3.2.8	K4	3

Question Number (#)	Correct Answer	LO	K-Level	Points
21	a	TA-3.3.1	K2	1
22	a, d	TA-3.3.2	K3	2
23	a	TA-3.3.3	K2	1
24	b	TA-3.4.1	K4	3
25	b	TA-4.2.1	K2	1
26	d	TA-4.2.1	K2	1
27	d	TA-4.2.2	K2	1
28	a, e	TA-4.2.3	K2	1
29	b	TA-4.2.3	K2	1
30	a	TA-4.2.4	K2	1
31	d	TA-4.2.5	K2	1
32	b	TA-4.2.5	K2	1
33	c, e	TA-4.2.6	K2	1
34	b, c	TA-4.2.7	K4	3
35	b	TA-4.2.7	K4	3
36	b	TA-5.2.1	K3	2
37	c	TA-5.2.1	K3	2
38	a, c	TA-5.2.2	K3	2
39	a, c	TA-6.2.1	K3	2
40	b	TA-6.3.1	K2	1

Test Analyst, Advanced Level
Sample Exam set A
Sample Exam – Answers

Answers

Question Number (#)	Correct Answer	Explanation / Rationale	Learning Objective (LO)	K-Level	Number of Points
1	b	a) Is not correct. Test analysis must start earlier, already during requirement specification in sequential lifecycle models b) Is correct. As per syllabus. This is the correct option of how testing activities should be aligned to the sequential lifecycle model phases c) Is not correct. As stated in the syllabus, there may be many differences in how the testing activities are aligned d) Is not correct. As stated in the syllabus a Test Analyst should be involved from the beginning in agile software development	TA-1.2.1	K2	1
2	d	a) Is not correct. This option ignores test conditions for risk mitigation and goes straight to test cases, and it is not specific about the objectives of test conditions b) Is not correct. This option ignores analysis of user stories and omits mention of desired coverage c) Is not correct. This option ignores test conditions altogether and goes straight to test cases d) Is correct. With risk mitigation added on to test conditions from the test basis	TA-1.3.1	K2	1
3	b	a) Is not correct. Yes, this is one of the good reasons, that is to verify that the test cases match the business processes and rules b) Is correct. Test cases should be created to comply with the organization's test strategy, not the other way around c) Is not correct. Yes, this is another good reason, namely that other testers should be able to understand and execute test cases d) Is not correct. Yes, developers need to be sure that they have the same understanding of the requirements as the testers in order to catch misunderstandings and also to participate in the optimization of tests	TA-1.4.1	K2	1

Test Analyst, Advanced Level
Sample Exam set A
Sample Exam – Answers

Question Number (#)	Correct Answer	Explanation / Rationale	Learning Objective (LO)	K-Level	Number of Points
4	a, d	a) Is correct. This is the best recommendation for project HIPPOS, the team has experience in testing and the availability of checklists would ensure a good level of coverage b) Is not correct. The testers do not have much testing experience, so logical level is not good as they need more detail on what to execute c) Is not correct. There are no arguments that support the same detailed level of documentation as the characteristics of the two test teams differ d) Is correct. The testers do not have much test experience and low-level test cases should achieve the high level of coverage e) Is not correct. There are no arguments that support the need for low-level test design for project HIPPOS as the testers are experienced and have access to checklists	TA-1.4.2	K4	3
5	d	a) Is not correct. The level of detail in the specifications will influence the choice of level of test design. For instance, if there no detailed requirements then low-level test design is not an option b) Is not correct. Audits to support regulatory compliance require low-level test design c) Is not correct. Testers without formal testing experience executing high-level test cases will not achieve acceptable levels of coverage d) Is correct. The sequence of phases is a functional requirement for B-OTC and will not influence the choice of level of test design	TA-1.4.2	K4	3

Question Number (#)	Correct Answer	Explanation / Rationale	Learning Objective (LO)	K-Level	Number of Points
6	c	a) Is not correct. Unscripted testing should be conducted in time boxed sessions b) Is not correct. If a risk-based test strategy is being used, risk priority order may dictate the execution order for the test cases c) Is correct. When creating the test execution schedule, dependencies between manual and automated test execution must be considered. d) Is not correct. The activities are not independent	TA-1.5.1	K2	1
7	c	a) Is not correct. Is a good suggestion but is a lower priority because the risk is lower. b) Is not correct. Is a good suggestion as the usability risk has a medium likelihood with high impact, but will not mitigate the risk until late in the development life cycle c) Correct. The usability risk has a medium likelihood with high impact. This is certainly the highest identified risk level, no matter which method is used to calculate the risk level, and it mitigates the risk early in the development life cycle d) Is not correct. This is a good suggestion but is a lower priority because the risk is lower	TA-2.1.1	K3	2

| 8 | b | The following are the equivalence classes for this question:

alcohol (2 classes):
(a1) ≤20 unit per week
(a2) >20 unit per week

filling in a "health risk assessment" (2 classes):
(h1) No
(h2) Yes

Participation in the health control programme:
(p1) No
(p2) Yes

BMI: (3 classes):
(b1) BMI ≤ 27.5
(b2) 27.5 < BMI <30
(b3) BMI ≥ 30

Smokers: (3 classes):
(s1) Not smoking
(s2) Smoking and joining a stop-smoking class
(s3) Smoking and not joining the class

Note that BMI and Smokers cases can only be tested when using p2, otherwise these parameters are not considered.

There are two variables that have 3 equivalence classes. Therefore, you have to have at least 3 tests. Since the second parameter (smoking) is only active when "program participation" = Yes", it means that none of the 3 values of Smoking will be tested when Participation = No. So you need 3 tests with Participation="Yes", and one more test to allow Participation to be | TA-3.2.1 | K4 | 3 |

Question Number (#)	Correct Answer	Explanation / Rationale	Learning Objective (LO)	K-Level	Number of Points
9	a	set to "No". The other parameters, having only 2 EC, will be covered by the same tests. Thus: a) Is not correct b) Is correct c) Is not correct d) Is not correct One needs the following 8 values to achieve 100% coverage of two-value boundary values (BVs): 0, 1, 40, 41, 150, 151, 300, 301 Existing tests cases have already covered the point values 12, 150, 151, 152 and 301. 12 and 152 are not two-value boundary values. So we have 3 BVs covered out of the 8. 3/8 = 37.5% Thus: a) Is correct b) Is not correct c) Is not correct d) Is not correct	TA-3.2.2	K4	3

Question Number (#)	Correct Answer	Explanation / Rationale	Learning Objective (LO)	K-Level	Number of Points
10	b, c	a) Is not correct. Due to the "don't care" values, the collapsed decision table needs less than 2³ rules. If we expanded the "don't care" values, to a full decision table, R3 would expand to two rules and R4 to four rules, which yields the correct number of 8 rules. b) Is correct. The "don't care" value for C2 in rule R3 is wrong. The rule must be split into two rules with the do not care value replaced with 'True' and 'False' respectively, because action A1 depends on condition C2. c) Is correct. A non-registered customer cannot have a registered credit card, so the system cannot provide card expiry information and the value should be a "N/A". d) Is not correct. According to the last sentence in the specification, direct debit is not allowed for non-registered customers, regardless of the purchase amount. Hence, the "don't care" value for condition C3 'Amount <= 500€' is correct e) Is not correct. In R2, C3 is TRUE, and option e) describes a situation where C3 is FALSE (purchase amount > 500€)	TA-3.2.3	K4	3

Test Analyst, Advanced Level
Sample Exam set A
Sample Exam – Answers

Question Number (#)	Correct Answer	Explanation / Rationale	Learning Objective (LO)	K-Level	Number of Points
11	d	a) Is not correct. The calculation of the difference between the data volume available and the file size is part of what the application does; it is not an input to the application. The inputs are the connectivity, file size and the available volume b) Is not correct. It is the difference between file size and available volume that is related to 20 KB c) Is not correct. Connection strength = 2 bars is only mandatory for two test cases covering the two rules R3 and R4 d) Is correct. The inputs are the connectivity, file size and the available volume. Given that the decision table is correct, it means that any given test case will only cover a single rule	TA-3.2.3	K4	3

| 12 | C | There are nine feasible 1-switches:

S1: Ready (Run) Running (Block) Blocked1
S2: Ready (Suspend) Blocked3 (Resume) Ready
S3: Running (Block) Blocked1 (Unblock) Ready
S4: Running (Block) Blocked1 (Suspend) Blocked2
S5: Blocked1 (Suspend) Blocked2 (Resume) Blocked1
S6: Blocked1 (Unblock) Ready (Suspend) Blocked3
S7: Blocked2 (Resume) Blocked1 (Unblock) Ready
S8: Blocked2 (Resume) Blocked1 (Suspend) Blocked2
S9: Blocked2 (Release) Blocked3 (Resume) Ready

There are also 4 other 1-switches:
Blocked1 (Unblock) Ready (Run) Running
Blocked1 (Unblock) Ready (Suspend) Blocked3
Blocked3 (Resume) Ready (Suspend) Blocked3
Blocked3 (Resume) Ready (Run) Running | TA-3.2.4 | K4 | 3 |

Question Number (#)	Correct Answer	Explanation / Rationale	Learning Objective (LO)	K-Level	Number of Points
		They are infeasible, since the state in the middle is "Ready", which forces the test to stop after reaching this state. Hence, we need to cover nine unique 1-switches S1-S9. Notice that four of them end in the "Ready" state, so no two of these four can be included in a single test case. Therefore, we need at least four test cases, and this is enough, for example: TC1: Ready (Suspend) Blocked3 (Resume) Ready TC2: Ready (Run) Running (Block) Blocked1 (Unblock) Ready TC3: Ready (Run) Running (Block) Blocked1 (Suspend) Blocked2 (Resume) Blocked1 (Suspend) Blocked2 (Release) Blocked3 (Resume) Ready TC4: Ready (Run) Running (Block) Blocked1 (Suspend) Blocked2 (Resume) Blocked1 (Unblock) Ready TC1 covers S2 TC2 covers in addition S1 and S3 TC3 covers in addition S4, S5, S8, S6, S9 TC4 covers in addition S7 Thus a) Is not correct b) Is not correct c) Is correct d) Is not correct			

| 13 | a | TA-3.2.4 | K4 | 3 |

[State diagram: IDLE ↔ READY (GPRS Attach / GPRS Detach), READY ↔ STAND-BY (Paging Request / READY Timer Expired), STAND-BY → IDLE (STANDBY Timer Expired)]

100% roundtrip coverage is achieved when all loops from any state back to the same state have been tested for all states at which loops begin and end. This loop cannot contain more than one occurrence of any particular state (except the initial/final one). Considering only READY state, following are the valid test cases:

1. READY > STAND-BY > READY
2. READY > IDLE > READY
3. READY > STAND-BY > IDLE > READY

Thus
a) Is correct
b) Is not correct
c) Is not correct
d) Is not correct

Question Number (#)	Correct Answer	Explanation / Rationale	Learning Objective (LO)	K-Level	Number of Points
14	c	a) Is not correct. Classification trees support the identification of equivalence partitions b) Is not correct. Classification trees support the identification boundary values c) Is correct. Classification trees do not support the identification of rules to be used in a decision table d) Is not correct. Classification trees support pairwise testing	TA-3.2.5	K2	1

Test Analyst, Advanced Level
Sample Exam set A
Sample Exam – Answers

Question Number (#)	Correct Answer	Explanation / Rationale	Learning Objective (LO)	K-Level	Number of Points
15	a	a) Is correct. We need at least 4 * 4 = 16 test cases to cover all combinations for "Material" and "Location". That 16 combinations are sufficient can be seen from the following table: | case #	Value 1	Value 2	Value 3
---	---	---	---
1	house	wood	city
2	house	concrete	suburb
3	house	brick	countryside
4	house	mixed	wilderness
5	semi-detached	wood	wilderness
6	semi-detached	concrete	countryside
7	semi-detached	brick	suburb
8	semi-detached	mixed	city
9	apartment	wood	countryside
10	apartment	concrete	wilderness
11	apartment	brick	city
12	apartment	mixed	suburb
13	cottage	wood	suburb
14	cottage	concrete	city
15	cottage	brick	wilderness
16	cottage	mixed	countryside | b) Is not correct. This is the result of the number of parameters multiplied by the choices (3 * 4). But we need at least 16 test cases, because this is the number of combinations for "Material" and "Location". c) Is not correct. Even for the full combination coverage (which subsumes pairwise) the required number of tests would be 4 * 4 * 4 = 64 cases, because this is the number of combinations for "Material" and "Location". d) Is not correct. This is 1-wise coverage. But we need at least 16 test cases, because this is the number of combinations for "Material" and "Location".	TA-3.2.6	K4	3

Question Number (#)	Correct Answer	Explanation / Rationale	Learning Objective (LO)	K-Level	Number of Points
16	c	To achieve the required coverage, we have to generate a set of test cases that covers all possible discrete combinations of each pair of input parameters. In this case the required coverage can be achieved with 9 test cases as shown in the following table: | TC	Language	Browser	OS
---	---	---	---
1	English	Br1	OpS1
2	English	Br2	OpS2
3	English	Br3	OpS3
4	French	Br1	OpS3
5	French	Br2	OpS1
6	French	Br3	OpS2
7	Japanese	Br1	OpS2
8	Japanese	Br2	OpS3
9	Japanese	Br3	OpS1 | Thus: a) Is not correct b) Is not correct c) Is correct d) Is not correct. The question requires the minimum number of test cases	TA-3.2.6	K4	3

Question Number (#)	Correct Answer	Explanation / Rationale	Learning Objective (LO)	K-Level	Number of Points
17	d	a) Is not correct. This is a situation with a test case for mainstream and one test case for the exceptions b) Is not correct. 1 is the minimum for mainstream but does not take into account the alternatives nor the exceptions c) Is not correct. The figure for this answer is calculated by adding test cases for the options with separate use cases to the correct number given in the correct answer d) Is correct. The correct number has one test case for the mainstream plus all the exception paths of which there are 4 E1's and 1 E2	TA-3.2.7	K4	3

Question Number (#)	Correct Answer	Explanation / Rationale	Learning Objective (LO)	K-Level	Number of Points
18	c	We need one test case for the main behavior. The remaining two alternative behaviors and two exceptions can be covered by three other test cases, so four test cases are needed in all, for example: TC1: main path: 1, 2, 3, 4, 5, 6, 7, 8, 9 TC2: forcing alternative 3a and exception E1: 1, 2, 3a, 2, E1 TC3: forcing alternative 8a: 1, 2, 3, 4, 5, 6, 7, 8a, 9 TC4: forcing E2: 1, 2, 3, E2 Note that we cannot cover the two alternative behaviors 3a and 8a and the two exceptions E1 and E2 with less than three test cases, because testing 8a requires to not invoke E1 and E2 (these events are before the step 8), and each exception must be tested with a separate test case, since the occurrence of an exception immediately ends the use case. Alternative 3a can be combined with the occurrence of E1 (or E2). Thus: a) Is not correct b) Is not correct c) Is correct d) Is not correct	TA-3.2.7	K4	3

Question Number (#)	Correct Answer	Explanation / Rationale	Learning Objective (LO)	K-Level	Number of Points
19	a, c	a) Is correct. State transition testing is appropriate because it will test for the correct navigation between the various screens. It will also enable management of the waiting list to be evaluated (e.g., transitions between application approved and waiting list) b) Is not correct. With the current specification, the use of decision table testing will only be of limited value c) Is correct. The specification mentions that an objective is to manage the numbers of players who can register for a particular team. Limits (i.e., numbers of registered players which a team can have) are to be enforced which may result in applicants being placed on a waiting list. The use of boundary value analysis is relevant for testing these limits. d) Is not correct. The required functionality of the app is to remain relatively simple. Use case testing could be applied, but it is less appropriate than state transition testing (answer a) and boundary value analysis (answer c). Note that the mention of usability testing in the scenario does not imply that use case testing should be applied as a test technique e) Is not correct. Nothing in the scenario indicates that pairwise testing would be appropriate. There is no explicit mention of combinatorial logic to be applied	TA-3.2.8	K4	3

Question Number (#)	Correct Answer	Explanation / Rationale	Learning Objective (LO)	K-Level	Number of Points
20	b, e	a) Is not correct. Although the system may be state-based there is no information about this in the scenario and the approach of building from an existing system suggests there may be minimal definition of state changes b) Is correct. Classification trees offer the opportunity to manage combinations of inputs effectively c) Is not correct. Some of the inputs are likely to be in partitions (e.g., colors) but these are unlikely to be ordered partitions because they identify alternatives, so boundary value analysis is not appropriate d) Is not correct. User case testing is appropriate to the likely development approach but would be based more on overall functional flow than on detailed combinations of inputs e) Is correct. The inputs exist in partitions (options) that are combined, so the combination of classification trees with equivalence partitioning would be an ideal choice	TA-3.2.8	K4	3

Test Analyst, Advanced Level
Sample Exam set A
Sample Exam – Answers

Question Number (#)	Correct Answer	Explanation / Rationale	Learning Objective (LO)	K-Level	Number of Points
21	a	a) Is correct. Experience-based techniques can be used as an option of more formal test techniques if the testers have enough experience and information about the system under test. Typically, this can happen in situations when there is time pressure, or the quality of documentation is poor or there is no documentation available b) Is not correct. Experience-based techniques can be used if no formal test techniques can be used, but it is not the only situation – they should be used to complement formal testing whenever it is possible c) Is not correct. Experience helps the tester to decide where to test more, but experience-based techniques do not necessarily improve the coverage since they are informal and coverage measurement is not always possible while using these techniques d) Is not correct. With the use of checklists, experience-based testing can be made more systematic and efficient, but if there is a requirement for the use of black-box test techniques, experience-based techniques cannot replace them. Even though this is partially correct, the question asks for the BEST option and thus this is not the correct answer	TA-3.3.1	K2	1
22	a, d	a) Is correct. Per the syllabus as a way to record results b) Is not correct. The pass/fail status of the session per the test charter should also be recorded c) Is not correct. Test cases are not normally defined for exploratory sessions d) Is correct. Per the syllabus as you will need this knowledge to figure out what to test since the problem is not defined e) Is not correct. This is likely to lead to lost results and no overall tracking	TA-3.3.2	K3	2

Question Number (#)	Correct Answer	Explanation / Rationale	Learning Objective (LO)	K-Level	Number of Points
23	a	a) Is correct. The defect-based test technique uses the typical defects identified for different types of software and programs as the source of test cases in order to find those specific type defects in the software under test b) Is not correct. Defect-based test techniques are mainly used in system testing, not in component testing c) Is not correct. Test cases are created by analyzing the defects typical for the system under test, not by analyzing the documentation of the system d) Is not correct. Defect-based testing is not a sub-category of black-box testing, since the specifications are not the basis of the test cases	TA-3.3.3	K2	1

Test Analyst, Advanced Level
Sample Exam set A
Sample Exam – Answers

Question Number (#)	Correct Answer	Explanation / Rationale	Learning Objective (LO)	K-Level	Number of Points
24	b	a) Is not correct. Defect-based testing is not mentioned at all. The team should use the taxonomy of common defect they built. For no 1 EP and BVA are mentioned while decision table would be more likely. Further black-box test techniques are proposed for security testing in no 4 where attack based, or defect-based test technique would be more suitable based on the scenario b) Is correct. This is the most likely proposal blending a number of techniques: It mentions both exploratory and defect-based testing, the latter of which is directly supported by the scenario, that states "the team …has as part of their retrospectives-built checklists of common defects…" and because the organization should have experience with the types of defects this type of application will exhibit. Further decision table testing is proposed which matches what is written in the scenario for no 1. Automated configuration testing is supported by the scenario for no 3 and so is checklist-based attacks for security testing in no 4 c) Is not correct. It is primarily wrong because there is no interoperability characteristics described in US1, but it could also have mentioned defect-based testing, since the scenario explicitly mentioned that the team has built a list of common defects d) Is not correct. It is not likely that black-box testing is applicable for no 1-4 in the scenario further there is nothing in no 1 that supports the use of state transition testing, instead decision table testing ought to have been mentioned	TA-3.4.1	K4	3

Test Analyst, Advanced Level
Sample Exam set A
Sample Exam – Answers

Question Number (#)	Correct Answer	Explanation / Rationale	Learning Objective (LO)	K-Level	Number of Points
25	b	a) Is not correct. Functional correctness is not the main focus because functionality which must be correct and accurate has been re-used from a similar application which has been in use for over 3 years. There is low risk that functional correctness is incorrect in the new application b) Is correct. A lack of functional completeness can be considered a risk because new functions are to be implemented and the users have not been involved in their definition. There is a risk that some required functionality has not been implemented c) Is not correct. Replaceability: this sub-characteristic of portability is clearly not appropriate d) Is not correct. Recoverability should be covered by a Technical Test Analyst and does not seem to be a main concern in this scenario	TA-4.2.1	K2	1
26	d	a) Is not correct. When the business expert could indicate correctness issues, this is not the aim of this exploratory testing session b) Is not correct. Accessibility is not mentioned as an objective of this test session, and business expert is probably not the best person to find accessibility issues c) Is not correct. Exploratory testing with a business expert is not the best way to check adaptability d) Is correct. The business expert can validate the appropriateness of the developed screen to allow a customer to choose a new mobile phone plan	TA-4.2.1	K2	1
27	d	a) Is not correct. The description relates to functional appropriateness b) Is not correct. Functional reliability testing is not a quality (sub-) characteristic c) Is not correct. The description relates to functional completeness d) Is correct. Functional correctness testing involves detecting incorrect handling of data or situations	TA-4.2.2	K2	1

Question Number (#)	Correct Answer	Explanation / Rationale	Learning Objective (LO)	K-Level	Number of Points
28	a, e	a) Is correct. Functional correctness tests can be conducted at any stage, and component testing is the earliest one b) Is not correct. Appropriateness testing is usually conducted during system testing but may also be conducted during the later stages of integration testing. Testing Appropriateness during acceptance testing is too late c) Is not correct. We are considering functional suitability, not interoperability d) Is not correct. Functional correctness tests can be conducted at any test level, so system testing is not the earliest one e) Is correct. Functional completeness for system integration testing may focus on the coverage of high-level business processes	TA-4.2.3	K2	1
29	b	a) Is not correct. Functional appropriateness is generally difficult to evaluate at a component level when you can only evaluate a small part of the system b) Is correct. Functional appropriateness testing is usually conducted during system testing, but may also be conducted during the later stages of integration testing c) Is not correct. Functional appropriateness testing should be conducted before acceptance tests when it could lead to huge coding rework d) Is not correct. Functional appropriateness should not be part of alpha or beta testing objectives. During alpha and beta testing, users will be more focused on usability and completeness issues (for instance)	TA-4.2.3	K2	1

Test Analyst, Advanced Level
Sample Exam set A
Sample Exam – Answers

Question Number (#)	Correct Answer	Explanation / Rationale	Learning Objective (LO)	K-Level	Number of Points
30	a	a) Is correct. The usability should be verified against the requirements and validated by the real users b) Is not correct. Validation should be done before release and by real users c) Is not correct. Heuristic evaluation is not a form of usability survey d) Is not correct. Usability cannot be verified by running a comparison with the existing unacceptable product	TA-4.2.4	K2	1
31	d	a) Is not correct. This is an interoperability issue with some websites b) Is not correct. This is an interoperability issue with a specific OS c) Is not correct. This is an interoperability issue with some browsers d) Is correct. This is a usability defect, not an interoperability defect	TA-4.2.5	K2	1
32	b	a) Is not correct. While usability is an important nonfunctional characteristic, especially in the client application, most of the electric scooter's users are young people and they usually have no problems with the application with the typical interface b) Is correct. It is easy to observe that the system must work in different environments; each part must cooperate with the other one; Therefore, interoperability is very important for this system c) Is not correct. As a Test Analyst, security testing should not be under your responsibility d) Is not correct. Performance may be a desired quality characteristic but there is no stated requirement and it would be anyhow less important than interoperability	TA-4.2.5	K2	1
33	c, e	a) Is not correct. This is a typical portability/adaptability defect b) Is not correct. This is a typical portability/installability defect c) Is correct. This is a typical accessibility defect d) Is not correct. This is a typical portability/ replaceability defect e) Is correct. This is a typical interoperability defect	TA-4.2.6	K2	1

Test Analyst, Advanced Level
Sample Exam set A
Sample Exam – Answers

Question Number (#)	Correct Answer	Explanation / Rationale	Learning Objective (LO)	K-Level	Number of Points
34	b, c	a) Is not correct. This addresses installability, which does not relate to the requirements b) Is correct. This test condition relates to usability aspects of requirement 1. "The user must be provided with an interface with which they can easily (do things) with the minimum number of steps" – this target in particular the efficiency aspects of usability c) Is correct. This test condition addresses the functional accuracy of the app's efficiency function, as stated in requirement 2 d) Is not correct. This addresses interoperability, which does not relate to the requirements e) Is not correct. This test condition addresses functionality which is not requested	TA-4.2.7	K4	3
35	b	a) Is not correct. R005 is a performance requirement and R006 is a technical portability requirement. Both must be taken in charge by a technical test analyst b) Is correct. R003 is an accessibility requirement and R004 is an adaptability requirement. All are in test analyst scope c) Is not correct. R007 is a security requirement. It must be taken in charge by a technical test analyst specialized in software security d) Is not correct. R004 is in the test analyst scope, but not R006 or R007 (see above justifications for details)			

Test Analyst, Advanced Level
Sample Exam set A
Sample Exam – Answers

Question Number (#)	Correct Answer	Explanation / Rationale	Learning Objective (LO)	K-Level	Number of Points
36	b	Evaluation of checklist items: 1. Is each requirement testable? — YES 2. Does each requirement have acceptance criteria listed? — NO 3. Does each requirement have a defined priority level? — NO 4. Are the requirements uniquely identified? — YES 5. Is the specification versioned? — NO 6. Is there traceability visible from each requirement to the business/marketing requirements? — NO 7. Is there traceability between the requirements and the use cases? — NO The question asks which of the items on the checklist are NOT met by the specification. Thus: a) Is not correct. Checklist item 1 is met b) Is correct. The set of checklist items [4, 6, 7] all three are not met c) Is not correct. Checklist item 5 is met d) Is not correct. Checklist item 5 is met	TA-5.2.1	K3	2
37	c	a) Is not correct. The requirement is not testable as there is no measurable criteria to determine if the requirement is met or not. The requirement has an identifier, but we cannot see its version number and there is no traceability to business or marketing requirement b) Is not correct. The requirement is not testable as there is no measurable criteria to determine if the requirement is met or not c) Is correct. There is an identifier, but none of the other items are respected d) Is not correct. The requirement is not testable	TA-5.2.1	K3	2

Question Number (#)	Correct Answer	Explanation / Rationale	Learning Objective (LO)	K-Level	Number of Points
38	a, c	a) Is correct. The story is not entirely written from the user's view. There are parts of the story which relate to what the loading machine does b) Is not correct. The feature is defined and distinct c) Is correct. "Loading machine is ready" cannot be tested because it is not stated what to check. Perhaps the cash entry slot for cash notes flashes. Perhaps the current balance is shown d) Is not correct. Priority 1 is explicitly stated e) Is not correct. The user story conforms to the standard structure	TA-5.2.2	K3	2
39	a, c	a) Is correct. The Test Analyst maintains the keywords and data to reflect changes made b) Is not correct. The Test Analyst does not modularize the automation scripts c) Is correct. The Test Analyst analyzes anomalies to determine if the problem is with the keywords, the input data, the automation script itself or with the application being tested d) Is not correct. The Test Analyst manually steps through the failed automated test with the same data to see if the failure is in the application itself e) Is not correct. If the cause of the anomaly cannot be found, the test is not removed from the automated regression testing pack	TA-6.2.1	K3	2
40	b	a) Is not correct. Test data preparation tools can "anonymize" data while still maintaining the internal integrity of that data b) Is correct. Test execution tools enable more tests to be run (not fewer) c) Is not correct. Test design tools can help the Test Analyst to choose the types of tests that are needed to obtain a targeted level of coverage d) Is not correct. Test execution tools enable the same tests to be repeated in many environments	TA-6.3.1	K2	1

Appendix: Answers to Additional Questions

Question Number (#)	Correct Answer	Explanation / Rationale	Learning Objective (LO)	K-Level	Number of Points
1	b	a) Is not correct. The test basis to be used may vary depending on the test level b) Is correct. Expected results may include data and environmental postconditions c) Is not correct. The process may be effective when combined with reviews and static analysis. In addition, dynamic analysis can only be performed during runtime and this is not always possible when designing test cases d) Is not correct. The required detailed test infrastructure requirements may be defined, although in practice these may not be finalized until test implementation	TA-1.4.3	K2	1
2	a	a) Is correct. The tasks listed are consistent with those given in the syllabus b) Is not correct. Implementing test automation and finalizing the test environments are test implementation activities c) Is not correct. Organizing tests into test suites is a test implementation activity, identifying the test conditions is a test analysis activity d) Is not correct. Analyzing the test basis is a test analysis activity, selecting test case design techniques is a test design activity	TA-1.6.1	K2	1

Printed in Great Britain
by Amazon